Apocalypse

Revealing Revelation

The Apocalypse in Revelation continues the narrative from the book of Daniel. It provides insight into the Churches of God, Satan's influence, and the events leading to the Last Days and World Wars. It also explains the causes of coming calamities and describes the return of the Messiah.

These passages offer significant detail, especially as their fulfillment becomes evident.

This End Time Prophecy is examined in detail, verse by verse, to ensure clarity for the reader. As the Last Days approach, its meaning will become increasingly clear.

By Pieter C Voges

Apocalypse

Disclaimer

© 2023, Author P. Voges

This eBook is designed to provide information and motivation to our readers. It may contain links to other websites or content belonging to or originating from third parties or links to websites and features. Such external links are not investigated, monitored, or checked for accuracy, adequacy, validity, reliability, availability or completeness.

All information in this eBooks is provided in good faith, however we make no representation or warranty of any kind, express or implied, regarding the accuracy, adequacy, validity, reliability, availability, or completeness of any information.

Photos are provided to assist in comprehension, but are not from actual events. They are from royalty free stock photos.

Grammarly gen AI was used to audit and enhance the writing for American English thereby improving the writing style for that market.

Apocalypse

Contents

Introduction

During the time Jesus Christ lived in Jerusalem, leaders of the global powers and religious authorities were given the opportunity to accept the Son of God and facilitate world peace. However, they collectively rejected Him. The general population also turned away from Him, with only a small group of disciples remaining faithful.

The prophecies delivered to Daniel were fulfilled. Knowledgeable Israelites from the East recognized the timing of the Messiah's first advent, as it was thoroughly documented. Daniel detailed the events impacting Israel and the Promised Land that led to the Messiah's first advent. Although God sent His Son to prevent further conflict and offered world leaders the chance to accept Him, these opportunities were ultimately rejected. Rather than embracing His message, world powers chose to execute Him.

At Christ's first advent, humanity was offered the opportunity to establish an ideal society, yet a lack of faith prevented it. Only a small number were willing to obey God and seek the Messiah's presence. The Pharisees and Sadducees negatively influenced the Jewish population, while the Roman Empire had the authority to permit Jesus Christ to establish the Kingdom of God in Jerusalem, but failed to uphold justice. The Herod family, who ruled in Jerusalem, also had the capacity to prevent what is considered one of history's greatest injustices.

Despite these opportunities, opposition to Jesus existed from the time of His birth. Some among the Arab population present in Jerusalem also called for the

Messiah's death and witnessed His crucifixion. These groups collectively missed the chance to prevent ongoing conflict.

Furthermore, approximately 660 years after the crucifixion, an alternative religion emerged among the Arab peoples, which denies the significance of the sacrifice made for humanity's understanding of our sinfulness. As a result, oppressive armies would persist in warfare until the world becomes prepared to accept the worship of God and the leadership of Jesus Christ. At that time, He will return and ultimately assume authority over all nations. Regrettably, collective failure must occur first before humanity will admit failure and turn to God and His Son, Jesus Christ.

Consequently, God provided a new set of prophecies through the apostle John. This book aims to clarify for readers the reasons behind God's allowance of these conflicts. Readers will be able to appreciate the fulfillment of biblical prophecies, many of which have already occurred, some that are unfolding now, and others that will continue to unfold until the return of Jesus Christ, the Messiah.

We will examine the relationship between the Ten Commandments and the first ten chapters of Revelation. The violation of these commandments leads to humanity's brokenness, which ultimately results in the events of the Apocalypse. The Bible demonstrates this correlation.

We will observe that the prophecies in Revelation have both immediate and long-term fulfillments, as illustrated by the principle of dual fulfillment. Ultimately, we will also explore the anticipated joy associated with the return of Jesus Christ. Many relevant scriptures were also added and discussed to clarify specific verses in Revelation.

Chapter 1

Identification of Powers

First Commandment:
> *"You shall have no other gods before Me."*
> (Exodus 20:3, MKJV)

(Worshipping multiple gods by multiple nations leads to disagreements, confrontations, and battles. Even different and false teachings and presentations of Jesus Christ lead to clashes between nations. World peace is possible if we all worship the same God the same way, according to God's Word.)

Why are there wars?

According to scripture, God did not intend for war. However, Adam and Eve chose to disregard God's command, setting a precedent that continues to this day. Jesus Christ warned that **false religions** would arise after His ascension, and these are often used to justify conflict.

> "And Jesus answering them began to say,
> Beware that no one deceive you.
> For many shall come in My name, saying,
> I AM, and shall deceive many.
> And when you shall hear of wars and
> rumors of wars, do not be troubled. For it

> must happen, but the end shall not be
> yet."
> (Mark 13:5-7, MKJV)

Many churches and pastors speak about the "I AM" and acknowledge Jesus as the Christ who was to come and will return. However, some present differing views, such as teaching that Jesus abolished the Commandments or did not die on the cross. Others deny that Jesus is the "I AM," the Christ, and the Son of God, recognizing Him only as a prophet and rejecting His resurrection and ascension. These teachings mislead many and contribute to conflict.

For this reason, the book of Revelation begins by identifying the true God and His Son, whom we are called to worship and follow. However, most people do not do so.

Revelation also contains messages for the Churches of God, offering encouragement and urging repentance to avoid losing salvation. Ultimately, the book describes evil empires and the wars they will instigate.

To distinguish truth from falsehood, the first chapter of Revelation offers guidance.

Revelation 1:1

Observe the hierarchical structure presented in the first verse and the explicit chain of command. The text suggests that, from the outset, certain churches and preachers may warrant scrutiny.

> "A Revelation of Jesus Christ, which God gave
> to Him to declare to His servants things which
> must shortly come to pass. And He signified it
> by sending His angel to His servant John,"
> (Revelation 1:1, MKJV)

Notice the hierarchy between individuals:

1) God the Father
2) Jesus Christ His Son
3) His Angel
4) The apostle John
5) His servants, the Churches of God

What can we deduct from this?

There is no mention of the Holy Spirit as a third person in this context. In the Bible, the Holy Spirit is described as the Spirit of God that motivates all members of the God Family. It is said to be poured out on the saints and resides within Christians, enabling them to love and keep the Ten Commandments. The Holy Spirit is not presented as a separate individual.

Jesus Christ is not depicted as God in a triune form in this context. Rather, He is presented as the subservient Son of God.

The angels serve under the authority of Jesus Christ. Jesus demonstrated greater power and righteousness through His life and sufferings on earth. He is regarded as the High Priest in the third Heaven at God's throne, directing the angels. These angels influence God's people on earth and, at times, can directly intervene, lead, and protect.

John is not identified as God, nor is the angel who delivered the message to John.

Revelation 1:2

Let's continue in Revelation:

"who bore record of the Word of God and of the testimony of Jesus Christ and of all the things that he saw."
(Revelation 1:2, MKJV)

Notice the following:

John possessed detailed knowledge of the Old Testament scriptures and testified about the Law of God and the messages conveyed by the prophets. He accompanied Jesus Christ throughout His three-year ministry in the Promised Land and comprehended His testimony. John witnessed the miracles performed by Jesus Christ and was fully convinced of the truth of his experiences and teachings. He also received several visions, which he regarded as authentic revelations rather than mere dreams.

Revelation 1:3

"Blessed is the one who reads and hears the Words of this prophecy, and the ones keeping the things written in it, for the time is near."
(Revelation 1:3, MKJV)

What is meant by the phrase "the time is near," given that Jesus has not yet returned?

The time is always near for us because human life is fragile and death may occur unexpectedly. The Apostles, who faced persecution from both civil and religious authorities, also lived with the awareness that their time was near. They believed that after death, they would be resurrected into the Kingdom of God at Christ's return.

Persecution for their faith was seen as a temporary difficulty, and part of their passage to eternal life.

> "Blessed are they who have been persecuted
> for righteousness sake! For theirs is the
> kingdom of Heaven.
> Blessed are you when men shall revile you
> and persecute you, and shall say all kinds of
> evil against you falsely, for My sake.
> Rejoice and be exceedingly glad, for your
> reward in Heaven is great. For so they
> persecuted the prophets who were before
> you."
> (Matthew 5:10-12, MKJV)

For the rest of humanity, it is important to understand the following: for the Eternal God, a day is like a thousand years. This concept has been recognized by God's prophets and apostles for millennia.

> "But, beloved, let not this one thing be
> hidden from you, that one day is with the
> Lord as a thousand years, and a thousand
> years as one day."
> (2 Peter 3:8, MKJV)

Therefore, the statement regarding the time of fulfillment "being near" should be understood as a broad assertion that holds true in multiple ways. For the general public and future generations, it may refer to a period of hundreds of years or more. However, because of sin and crime, death can occur at any time; thus, the time is always near.

Revelation 1:4

A further careful investigation is required to identify who is being mentioned in this verse.

"John to the seven churches which are in Asia. Grace to you and peace from Him who is and who was and who is coming; and from the seven spirits which are before His throne;"
(Revelation 1:4, MKJV)

The apostle John serves as the earthly messenger, tasked with conveying the message entrusted to him for the churches of God. The source of this message and the identity of the figure John references warrant careful examination.

The message originates from the One who secured grace for humanity through a supreme and unparalleled sacrifice. This figure existed prior to the earthly ministry, currently serves as High Priest in Heaven, and is anticipated to return at the Second Advent.

Revelation 1:5

He is identified as Jesus the Christ:

"even from Jesus Christ the faithful Witness, the First-born from the dead and the Ruler of the kings of the earth. To Him who loved us and washed us from our sins in His own blood,"
(Revelation 1:5, MKJV)

We need to pause at this verse and see it in light of other verses. The designation of Jesus as the ruler of the kings of the earth should be interpreted in light of other scriptural passages, as this is not presently the case. Rather, this statement is prophetic. In scripture, God often refers to future events as though they have already occurred, reflecting decisions made in Heaven that will ultimately be fulfilled.

> "(as it has been written, "I have made you a father of many nations") --before God, whom he believed, who makes the dead live, and calls the things which **do not exist as though they do exist**."
> (Romans 4:17, MKJV) [Emphasis mine]

God the Father, through Jesus Christ His Son, has previously offered to govern or provide guidance to various world leaders; however, all rejected the authority of the God Family.

God extended guidance to Nebuchadnezzar during his campaign to capture Jerusalem. God caused Nebuchadnezzar to endure hardship to prompt recognition of divine sovereignty, yet Nebuchadnezzar ultimately rejected God and lost his position. See Daniel 4 and 5.

God dispatched Jonah the prophet to Nineveh to urge repentance, and the city responded. The king of Nineveh admitted his transgressions against the God of Israel and repented, demonstrating a commitment to worship God, at least temporarily. This act preserved Nineveh.

> "For word came to the king of Nineveh, and he arose from his throne. And he laid his robe

from him, and covered himself with sackcloth, and sat in ashes."
(Jonah 3:6, MKJV)

Even Saul, the king of Israel, eventually ceased worshipping God and sought guidance from a woman who acted as a medium between demons and people. These demons possessed knowledge of God's will and historical events up to that point, deceiving King Saul. As a result, God ended Saul's reign and subsequently his life, as described in 1 Samuel 28. In the seventh millennium, it is prophesied that the Messiah will rule from Jerusalem until the fulfillment of all things, as referenced in 1 Corinthians 15:22-28.

Revelation 1:6

"and made us kings and priests to God and His Father, to Him be glory and dominion forever and ever. Amen."
(Revelation 1:6, MKJV)

The apostle John was honouring and recognising the reality of what Jesus achieved for him and others. At the beginning of the ages of the Kings of Israel, God allowed the separation of Church and State, but that is not ideal for God, as can be seen from the failures of many kings of Israel.

Therefore the real apostles and others that followed would be tested and proven to be incorruptible, and would be granted to rule in Jesus Christ's Name, to be both kings and priests. In the resurrection at Christ's return, church and state will be united again under these proven leaders.

> "And Jesus said to them, Truly I say to you that you who have followed Me, in the regeneration, when the Son of Man shall sit in the throne of His glory, you also shall sit on twelve thrones, judging the twelve tribes of Israel."
> (Matthew 19:28, MKJV)

This will be fulfilled one day. That was the sure faith for those that sacrificed their lives for Jesus Christ. That is the sure prophecy for those that keep the Commandments and followed Jesus in His understanding of the Law of God and the true Worship of our Heavenly Father. When Jesus returns, He will award those who sacrificed to stay true to the Covenant even in the face of opposition from corrupt leaders and wayward society.

Revelation 1:7

> "Behold, He comes with the clouds, and every eye will see Him, and those who pierced Him will see Him, and all the kindreds of the earth will wail because of Him. Even so, Amen."
> (Revelation 1:7, MKJV)

The second advent of Messiah will be with power. He has already been proven as subservient and loving, even to His death. His appearance will be supernatural. Humankind will know that He came to be our Messiah and stop all wars and corruption.

Many state and religious leaders will be shocked, but this time there is nothing that can stop the merciful and glorious rule over Jerusalem, then Israel, and spreading throughout the world. This was promised.

"And then the sign of the Son of Man shall appear in the heavens. And then all the tribes of the earth shall mourn, and they shall see the Son of Man coming in the clouds of the heaven with power and great glory."
(Matthew 24:30, MKJV)

In the world the piercing of Jesus continues. Politicians resist His rule. Many vilify the followers of Jesus. Evangelists are jailed and killed in many countries. Pastors are persecuted in some former "Christian" countries for refusing to marry homosexuals. Some Hollywood "stars" use His Name in vain a thousand times a day! All over the world Jesus is still "being pierced". What a shock it will be when the world sees His supernatural return!

Revelation 1:8

"I am the Alpha and Omega, the Beginning and the Ending, says the Lord, who is and who was and who is to come, the Almighty."
(Revelation 1:8, MKJV)

Some may misunderstand this verse and make a wrong identification. This verse is often used to suggest that Jesus Christ is very God, the same being as the Father. For many it seems to prove the Trinity doctrine. This way many scriptures are discounted, and the truth becomes hidden. But it must be seen in the light of all scriptures that precede this statement. A quick discussion is warranted:

Everything was created through Jesus Christ, and for Him.

"All things came into being **through** Him, and without Him not even one thing came into being that has come into being."
(John 1:3, MKJV) [Emphasis mine]

Jesus was the beginning of God's creation plan. The Father fully trusts His Son, and gave everything into his hands. The Bible clearly shows a relationship between two powerful beings, with Christ being subservient to His Father, the Most High God.

"The Father loves the Son and has given all things into His hand"
(John 3:35, MKJV)

Even everlasting life has been given to the Son after his crucifixion and resurrection. It is a gift that was given. This shows a relationship between the two!

"For as the Father has life in Himself, so He has given to the Son to have life within Himself,
and has given Him authority to execute judgment also, because He is the Son of Man."
(John 5:26-27, MKJV)

Jesus will even judge between who lives forever and who are unrepentant and will be thrown into the lake of fire to be exterminated, because it was specifically given to Him. After such a long time of complete subservient obedience and love, Jesus acts just like God the Father, knowing His Will completely. Hence the Father can trust Jesus to fulfil His divine Will.

"who is the image of the invisible God, the
First-born of all creation.
For all things were created in Him, the things
in the heavens, and the things on the earth,
the visible and the invisible, whether thrones
or dominions or principalities or powers, all
things were created through Him and for
Him."
(Colossians 1:15-16, MKJV)

Jesus the Christ, our Messiah, is not part of a Triune God. The Trinity doctrine is a fourth century construct of the Roman Empire to please Emperor Constantine. Many books have been written about how it entered the Roman church. However, no rabbi or apostle ever taught such a concept, and the original manuscripts of the Bible did not teach it.

Jesus existed before Adam. Therefor He was before Adam and Eve. Jesus willingly gave up His prior life with almighty God to come to the earth as a flesh and blood human being. He was crucified and resurrected, and many followers worship and follow Him. Therefor He is. And He will return when the world is at the point of self-destruction and is desperate for a supernatural power to provide salvation out of the mess that humankind have caused. Therefor He is to come. And He will be mighty over all rulers, governments and armies. God the Father has given it all to him.

This completes the introduction and identification of our Messiah that will save us out of the Apocalypse.

Revelation 1:9-12

John continues to explain his own situation as he writes what he was told to write.

"I, John, who also am your brother and companion in the affliction, and in the kingdom and patience of Jesus Christ, was in the island that is called Patmos, for the Word of God and for the testimony of Jesus Christ. I came to be in the Spirit in the Lord's day and heard behind me a great voice, as of a trumpet,
saying, I am the Alpha and Omega, the First and the Last. Also, What you see, write in a book and send it to the seven churches which are in Asia: to Ephesus, and to Smyrna, and to Pergamos, and to Thyatira, and to Sardis, and to Philadelphia, and to Laodicea.
And I turned to see the voice that spoke with me."
(Revelation 1:9-12, MKJV)

Who was the Logos, the spokesperson who is authorised to provide the prophecies of the apocalypse? The angel communicating with John identified the authority that gave him these messages.

Revelation 1:13-16

"And having turned, I saw seven golden lampstands. And in the midst of the seven lampstands I saw One like the Son of man, clothed with a garment down to the feet, and tied around the breast with a golden band.
His head and hair were white like wool, as white as snow. And His eyes were like a flame of fire.
And His feet were like burnished brass having been fired in a furnace. And His voice was like the sound of many waters.
And He had seven stars in His right hand, and out of His mouth went a sharp two-edged sword. And His face was like the sun shining in its strength."
(Revelation 1:13-16, MKJV)

The angel showed John the risen Jesus Christ, who is alive and ruling from the right hand of God. Jesus is still fulfilling His mission to humankind, for He now also has experience as a flesh and blood human being, and is the perfect agent between almighty God and failing humanity.

Revelation 1:17-20

Now Jesus personally communicated with John:

"And when I saw Him, I fell at His feet as dead. And He laid His right hand upon me,

saying to me, Do not fear, I am the First and the Last,
and the Living One, and I became dead, and behold, I am alive for ever and ever, Amen. And I have the keys of hell and of death.
Write the things which you have seen, and the things which are, and the things which shall be after this,
the mystery of the seven stars which you saw in My right hand and the seven golden lampstands. The seven stars are the angels of the seven churches, and the seven lampstands which you saw are the seven churches."
(Revelation 1:17-20, MKJV)

John recognized the seven churches established by the apostle Paul, located along a mail route extending from Jerusalem and returning. Other churches existed in nearby towns, including small groups meeting in homes. Notably, the churches in Jerusalem and Rome are not included in this list. At this time, Jerusalem was under Roman occupation, the Temple had been destroyed, and church leadership had fled to the mountains of Petra. Many members had relocated, and some apostles may have already been killed. As a result, these seven churches likely represented the core of Christianity during this period.

These churches made significant contributions, but further improvement was needed. Jesus provided urgent guidance, as they still had much to learn. The following two chapters are addressed to these churches, emphasizing that their ability to overcome shortcomings was essential for future developments. If they repented and strengthened their service to God through the ministry of Jesus Christ, they were destined for greatness in the seventh millennium.

Summary

It is essential to recognize who delivered the message of the Apocalypse. Understanding the Messiah who made this prophecy possible is crucial. Without Jesus' willingness to become human, overcome adversity, and demonstrate complete loyalty to God and love for humanity, salvation would not be possible.

Jesus Christ, the Son of God, possesses the love and obedience needed to restore what was lost in the Garden of Eden. He overcame Satan as a human, subject to death like all of us. Through His unwavering love, loyalty, and obedience, He secured the path to salvation as our sacrifice and High Priest. Jesus fully understands how to mediate between us and God, which qualified Him to reveal this prophecy to us.

Understanding Jesus Christ, the Son of God, is essential to unlocking the mystery of Revelation. John wisely emphasized this at the outset. Through this message, we are shown both humanity's failings and the promise of future hope. Ultimately, salvation will be available to all.

The next two chapters reveal a threefold prophetic fulfillment of God's inspired message. First, the seven Churches existed along a mail route in Asia and received these messages directly. Second, these Churches represent seven historical eras. Third, remnants of the last four eras will persist worldwide at the end. This will be discussed further in Revelation 2 and 3.

Chapter 2

Churches of God

Second Commandment:
"You shall not make to yourselves any graven image, or any likeness of anything that is in the heavens above, or that is in the earth beneath, or that is in the water under the earth.
You shall not bow yourself down to them, nor serve them. For I Jehovah your God am a jealous God, visiting the iniquity of the fathers upon the sons to the third and fourth generation of those that hate me,
and showing mercy to thousands of those that love Me and keep My commandments."
(Exodus 20:4-6, MKJV)

(Worshippers are told not to create representations of their ideas about God or Jesus Christ. It will invariably lead to misunderstandings and, hence, disagreements. The mental image of God will change and improve over time with scriptural studies until we all have a unified concept of God, leading to peace).

Before examining the messages to the Churches of God, it is important to clearly identify them. While many churches exist, not all represent the Churches of God.

Apostasy began in the first century and worsened over time. By the fourth century, the church at Rome was influenced by the Roman Emperor, who imposed altered doctrines throughout the Empire, incorporating many pagan ideas and practices. Therefore, the messages in chapters 2 and 3 do not address the church at Rome, its offshoots from the Middle Ages, or later reformist churches, as the reformation was incomplete.

It is essential to understand the core doctrines of the first-century Churches of God and the pagan environment in which they developed. This context will clarify the messages in Revelation chapters two and three.

Identification of the Churches of God

The Old and New Covenants both represent agreements between humans and God to uphold the Ten Commandments. The primary differences are the method of enactment, the role of the High Priest, and the reasons for obedience. However, the Commandments remain eternal.

In prophecy, Israel is depicted as the "woman," and after Christ's arrival, the Church assumes this role. Satan, referred to as the dragon, attempted to destroy both the "woman" and the Messiah who emerged from her, but was unsuccessful.

> "And the dragon was enraged over the woman, and went to make war with the rest of her seed, who keep the **commandments of God** and have the testimony of Jesus Christ." (Revelation 12:17, MKJV) [Emphasis mine]

The Churches of God have consistently observed the Commandments, including the Fourth Commandment to worship on the Sabbath, the seventh day. Their growth was largely due to the apostle Paul's evangelising. Although the Roman Empire ultimately favored and later enforced worship on the first day of the week, these original Churches of God maintained First Century Theology. Sunday churches did not exist at that time. Please consider the practices of the original Churches of God:

"And the Jews having gone out of the synagogue, the nations begged that these words might be preached to them the next sabbath.
And the synagogue being broken up, many of the Jews and of the devout proselytes followed Paul and Barnabas; who, speaking to them, persuaded them to continue in the grace of God.
And on the coming sabbath day almost all the city came together to hear the Word of God."
(Acts 13:42-44, MKJV)

Hence the reader must understand that the original Christian churches were beset by temptations of the gentile converts to return to the paganism of the Sunday religions on the one hand, and also for the Jewish converts to return to the Old Testament, and even the practices of the Pharisees.

Messages to the Churches of God

At first the messages from God goes out to His Churches. Jesus would reveal to them what God the Father was planning to allow as man's kingdoms fail.

Humans could have built eternal kingdoms, but the rejection of God's Commandments and Laws leads to crime and eventually wars and destruction. Hence the prophecies of human attempts and failures continue. God therefor revealed how kingdoms will fail, and how suburbs will disintegrate and cities eventually be laid waste.

"No longer do I call you servants, for the servant does not know what his master does. But I have called you friends, for all things that I have heard from My Father I have made known to you."
(John 15:15, MKJV)

The messages to the Churches of God have a threefold fulfilment, as can be seen in other prophecies as well. Firstly it goes out to seven actual physical Churches in physical locations. Secondly the successes and failures on a spiritual level can - and have - happened in the Churches of God at various stages throughout the ages. And thirdly, in the world today, there may be various main international groups preaching to the world through various media and methods, and one or more of these spiritual descriptions may apply to these worldwide organisations. Therefor some of these messages can be seen as End Time prophecies, as we will find out.

From Jerusalem a mail route went out and curved back to Jerusalem through Asia Minor. Seven places are mentioned and seven messages are given. These churches were in the country currently called Turkey.

The apostle John was held captive on the isle of Patmos, which is in the Mediterranean Sea. Therefor mail would go out from Patmos by ship to Ephesus and on to the other cities and churches mentioned.

For a map see the link below:

http://www.about-jesus.org/seven-churches-revelation-map.htm

Seven is the number of perfection and completion in the Bible. For instance, God renewed the surface of the earth over seven days during the Creation Week, and He said it was perfect.

"You send forth Your Spirit, they are created; and You renew the face of the earth."
(Psalms 104:30, MKJV)

See the book on Harmonizing the Creation Week and Science

https://www.amazon.com/gp/product/B08DNP24BL?ref_=dbs_m_mng_rwt_calw_tkin_10&storeType=ebooks

This shows that through the Churches of God, the Creator will renew the saints and make them perfect. The route going out and curving back to Jerusalem also shows that the saints will go out into the world and eventually will come back to Jerusalem at the resurrection and return of Messiah. Jerusalem was given to Jesus Christ by God the Father, and Jesus will return to His inheritance at the Second Advent.

Revelation 2:1-7:
Ephesus – First message

The first Church established by Paul in the region or province apparently was at Ephesus. It served as a springboard to the rest of the province.

"To the angel of the church of Ephesus write:
He who holds the seven stars in His right
hand, who walks in the midst of the seven
golden lampstands, says these things.
I know your works and your labor and your
patience, and how you cannot bear those who
are evil. And you tried those pretending to be
apostles, and are not, and have found them
liars.
And you have borne, and have patience, and
for My name's sake you have labored and
have not fainted.
But I have against you that you left your first
love.
Therefore remember from where you have
fallen, and repent, and do the first works, or
else I will come to you quickly and will remove
your lampstand out of its place unless you
repent.
But you have this, that you hate the deeds of
the Nicolaitans, which I also hate.
He who has an ear, let him hear what the
Spirit says to the churches. To him who
overcomes I will give to eat of the Tree of Life,
which is in the midst of the paradise of God."
(Revelation 2:1-7, MKJV)

Jesus warns that He has power over the churches. He moves and inspires their formation, but if sin is not removed, He can again allow them to disintegrate. He commends them for their work and patience, and that they were willing to remove false leaders (apostles) who misled members (disciples).

However, the road to salvation is not an easy one in this evil world, and Christians can grow weary and possibly lose sight of the glorious coming Kingdom of God that will be established by Jesus Christ at His second advent. The chance to be in the first resurrection and live forever can be lost. The chance of being leaders forever in the coming Kingdom of God can evaporate. This is explained in later chapters, particular chapter 20. The love is for those who worship God and keep His Commandments, as John explained previously.

> "By this we know that we love the children of God, whenever we love God and keep His commandments.
> For this is the love of God, that we keep His commandments, and His commandments are not burdensome."
> (1 John 5:2-3, MKJV)

This also is an indication for members concerning leaders who lose their way and begin to teach people that the Law is done away, and that people can disregard the Commandments. Members should isolate such leaders. The Commandments will always stand. The reason and way to come to repentance and receive forgiveness have changed when the New Testament was established, but the Covenant still involves the keeping of the Commandments.

Without the Commandments a church can descent into spiritual darkness and lawlessness.

The deeds of the Nicolaitans are probably those done by Nicolas. There have been many occasions of leadership that lost their way to preach the easy gospel, saying that the Commandments are done away, and all sin are forgiven continuously while people continue in their sin! Nicholas was from Antioch, as the Bible explains.

"And the saying pleased all the multitude. And they chose Stephen, a man full of faith and of the Holy Spirit, and Philip, and Prochorus, and Nicanor, and Timon, and Parmenas, and **Nicholas, a proselyte of Antioch**."
(Acts 6:5, MKJV) [Emphasis mine]

The church in Pergamos mentioned in Revelation actually tolerated these followers of Nicholas. Notice later in Revelation 2 in the message to the church in Pergamos:

"But I have a few things against you, because you have there those who hold the teachings of Balaam, who taught Balak to cast a stumbling-block before the sons of Israel, to eat things sacrificed to idols and to commit fornication.
So you also have those who hold the teaching of the Nicolaitans, which thing I hate."
(Revelation 2:14-15, MKJV)

These things were specifically prohibited even among gentiles in the New Testament! Today we also see the sin of gay priesthood and gay marriages in churches! This is exactly the fornication espoused by the Nicolaitans. St Nicolas had to be banished or the membership would lose their way and salvation!

> "Therefore my judgment is that we do not
> trouble those who have turned to God from
> among the nations,
> but that we write to them that they should
> abstain from pollutions of idols, and from
> fornication, and from things strangled, and
> from blood."
> (Acts 15:19-20, MKJV)

So it seems that Nicholas lost his way and started to mislead members. The church in Ephesus correctly had such wayward leaders removed, but the church in Pergamos tolerated them!

Today we see many "Christian" churches allowing "gay priests!" Many churches bow before the politics enforcing acceptance of the LGBQ+ doctrines. This is obviously not Christian! This is not Biblical. Jesus Christ states that He hates the deeds of these Nicolaitans. Those who avoided the falling away can still reach eternal life.

Revelation 2:8-11:
Smyrna – Second Message

> "And to the angel of the church in Smyrna
> write: The First and the Last, who became
> dead and lived, says these things:
> I know your works and tribulation and
> poverty (but you are rich), and I know the
> blasphemy of those saying themselves to be

Jews, and are not, but are the synagogue of
Satan.
Do not at all fear what you are about to suffer.
Behold, the Devil will cast some of you into
prison, so that you may be tried. And you will
have tribulation ten days. Be faithful to death,
and I will give you the crown of life.
He who has an ear, let him hear what the
Spirit says to the churches. He who
overcomes will not be hurt by the second
death."
(Revelation 2:8-11, MKJV)

Jesus is again identified as the one that was
crucified but resurrected, and who pre-existed, and who is
the heir of the earth, and will return and reign.

In history books it is indicated that Polycarp was the
Bishop of the Church of God in Smyrna. However, the
Roman governor was keen to enforce the state religion,
which basically was relics of the worship of the sun, on
Sunday. The Jews were in danger of persecution due to the
differences. Most notably would be the keeping of the
Saturday Sabbath, which the Christians also kept. Add to
that the fact that since Christians worship the Creator God,
they would also follow Jesus through whom everything was
created, instead of the created sun. Hence Christians
became enemy of the state by default. Even some of the
Jews did not stay in their worship, but compromised and
turned on the Christians. They reported Christians and so in
effect became followers of Satan.

In the first verse Christians were reminded of the
sufferings and death of Jesus the Christ, who was
resurrected and lives forever. This could be a path for some
of the followers of Jesus as well if they keep their faith.

They can be assured that they will be in the first resurrection as indicated in Revelation 20, and will be directly resurrected into eternal glorified bodies that are of a nature that does not get old nor will ever die or feel pain again. They will not be in subsequent resurrections into physical earthly bodies nor will face the final death, but will be in the first and glorious resurrection.

> "But the fearful, and the unbelieving, and the abominable, and murderers, and whoremongers, and sorcerers, and idolaters, and all liars, will have their part in the Lake burning with fire and brimstone, which is the second death."
> (Revelation 21:8, MKJV)

This tribulation in Smyrna would last ten years, probably till the Roman governor died or was replaced. From scriptures we can often see that a prophetic day refers to a year in human terms. Hence we can assume that the "ten days" refer to ten years of persecution of this church in Smyrna. Notice this principle explained elsewhere:

> "And when you have fulfilled them, lie again on your right side, and you shall bear the iniquity of the house of Judah forty days; **a day for a year; a day for a year**, I have set for you."
> (Ezekiel 4:6, MKJV) [Emphasis mine]

It would have been a torrid time for Christians under the godless governor. However, those that kept their faith would prove such a ruler to be like a beast as explained in other sections of Revelation. Such ruthless and misguided leaders would eventually die and ultimately one day be in the Judgment day. Yet those he persecuted will ultimately rule with Christ at His second advent in the coming Kingdom of God.

Revelation 2:12-17:
Pergamos – Third Message

"And to the angel of the church in Pergamos write: He who has the sharp sword with two edges says these things.
I know your works, and where you live, even where Satan's seat is.
And you hold fast My name and have not denied My faith, even in those days in which Antipas was My faithful martyr, who was slain among you, where Satan dwells.
But I have a few things against you, because you have there those who hold the teachings of Balaam, who taught Balak to cast a stumbling-block before the sons of Israel, to eat things sacrificed to idols and to commit fornication.
So you also have those who hold the teaching of the Nicolaitans, which thing I hate.
Repent! But if not I will come to you quickly, and will fight with them by the sword of My mouth.
He who has an ear, let him hear what the Spirit says to the churches. To him who overcomes I will give to eat of the hidden manna, and will give to him a white stone,

and in the stone a new name written, which
no man knows except he who receives it."
(Revelation 2:12-17, MKJV)

On a hill near Pargamos, many heathen temples were built. Citizens would go and offer unclean meat to be burnt for the pagan gods, and eat it. Typically some had temple whores leading to the clear indication from God's Word that they were committing fornication. It was correctly seen by Jews and Christians alike that this hill was Satan's seat.

Verse 13 indicates that they held on to the name of God and of Jesus Christ, and faith in Jesus as well as the faith Jesus had in His Father.

Unfortunately the Church of God in that city compromised grossly, and a warning went out to them to repent or lose their potential status in God's Kingdom. That church could also disintegrate. Balak misled Israel in the Old Testament. In the New Testament era the Nicolaitans, followers of Nicholas of Antioch, taught them to compromise and deceived many members of the Church in clear violation of the Law and instructions of Church leadership from Jerusalem.

"Therefore my judgment is that we do not
trouble those who have turned to God from
among the nations,
but that we write to them that they should
**abstain from pollutions of idols, and from
fornication**, and from things strangled, and
from blood."
(Acts 15:19-20, MKJV) [Emphasis mine]

There is a way to twist the teachings of Paul to allow members to continue in sin.

"What then? Shall we sin because we are not under Law, but under grace? **Let it not be**!" (Romans 6:15, MKJV) [Emphasis mine]

Paul describes the process of forgiveness of past sin and motivation to cease from sin. It is the sin in people that caused them to crucify Christ! The purpose was not to allow sin to continue! We cannot crucify Christ over and over again!

"And think of the long-suffering of our Lord as salvation (as our beloved brother Paul also has written to you according to the wisdom given to him
as also in all his letters, speaking in them of these things; in which are some things hard to be understood, which the unlearned and unstable pervert, as also they do the rest of the Scriptures, to their own destruction). Therefore, beloved, knowing beforehand, beware lest being led away with the error of the lawless, you fall from your own steadfastness."
(2 Peter 3:15-17, MKJV)

Members and leadership of this church was deceived and compromised with the paganism from the nearby hill. Jesus was going to send someone to preach sternly to them in an attempt to save them from final rejection. Those who repent from the sin of the pagans would be granted more understanding and knowledge of the Kingdom of God. It would be like manna that comes from Heaven, to feed them. If they do repent, they would be given a white stone indicating access to the New Jerusalem, and a new name indicating new status and seniority in the coming Kingdom of God.

If they don't repent from the paganism creeping into their lives and worship, their labour would be in vain! They will not understand the spiritual manna from Heaven. They will lose knowledge of the Kingdom of God. They will not be usable to Christ at His return. They will not be in the first resurrection. Such churches will also lose the name "Church of God".

Revelation 2:18-29: Thyatira – Fourth Message

"And to the angel of the church in Thyatira write: The Son of God, He who has His eyes like a flame of fire and His feet like burnished metal, says these things:
I know your works and love and service and faith and your patience, and your works; and the last to be more than the first.
But I have a few things against you because you allow that woman Jezebel to teach, she saying herself to be a prophetess, and to cause My servants to go astray, and to commit fornication, and to eat idol-sacrifices.
And I gave her time that she might repent of her fornication, and she did not repent.
Behold, I am throwing her into a bed, and those who commit adultery with her into great affliction, unless they repent of their deeds.

And I will kill her children with death. And all
the churches will know that I am He who
searches the reins and hearts, and I will give
to every one of you according to your works.
But to you I say, and to the rest in Thyatira,
as many as do not have this doctrine, and
who have not known the depths of Satan, as
they speak, I will put on you no other burden.
But that which you have, hold fast until I
come.
And he who overcomes and keeps My works to
the end, to him I will give power over the
nations.
And he will rule them with a rod of iron, as
the vessels of a potter they will be broken to
pieces, even as I received from My Father.
And I will give him the Morning Star.
He who has an ear, let him hear what the
Spirit says to the churches."
(Revelation 2:18-29, MKJV)

Jesus Christ, the Son of God, was given power and
glory for His unwavering love and obedience. Jesus
acknowledges the work done by this church. However, they
allowed a false prophetess to mislead the Church!

Jezebel is identified as the pagan worshipper that
misled one of the kings of Israel. She was a pagan queen,
and after marriage to the king of Israel, she simply
continued in her wayward sinful life, and caused the rot to
spread to Israel. She even directly opposed true prophets of
God. Her evil deeds are well recorded in the books on the
kings of Israel:

"And as if it had been a light thing for him to walk in the sins of Jeroboam the son of Nebat, he also took **Jezebel**, the daughter of Eth-baal king of the Sidonians, for a wife. And he went and served Baal, and worshiped him."
(1 Kings 16:31, MKJV) [Emphasis mine]

Jezebel caused a major falling away from the true worship in Israel. The same type of character was present in this church of God, causing a major falling away.

The instructions in the New Testament are clear, but many churches ignore that:

"Let your women be silent in the churches; for it is not permitted to them to speak, but to be in subjection, as the Law also says."
(1 Corinthians 14:34, MKJV)

This woman was given time to repent, as affliction came to her. Her "church" suffered spiritual and physical affliction, to make them think and search the truth of God's Word. This shows the mercy and grace extended to wayward members and leaders, but not forever. Her wayward "church" spawned more wayward groups and churches, but they were killed. They lost all chance of salvation. Such churches disintegrated in that town, and wherever they spread their false worship.

Christ commended those who proved her wrong and did not follow her false leaders. They had no further burden but to suffer the loss of those who compromised, and to persevere in the struggle to search scripture to prove what the true worship was. They were to hold on to that truth till the end. Those who could not be swayed by false leaders that crept in unawares proved their worth. They will one day be in the resurrection to lead others in the coming Kingdom of God. They are strong like iron, unmovable in the true doctrine and faith. They have the power and strength of character to prove the wayward leaders wrong, and eventually break their false fellowship, which is not according to the knowledge from God's Word. They will rule with Christ at His return.

Church Eras

Consider the possibility that these seven messages to seven churches also refer to the fact that there will be seven Church eras of worldwide growth which may render some members to sustain those eras till Jesus returns. Thyatira would then be the forth Church that will be oppressed but members and their extended families may keep the spirit of that era alive in various places of the world till Jesus comes. Hence the following inscription rings true:

"hold fast until I come"

The Church suffered the persecution that came in Europe during the Dark Middle Ages. Ultimately gross error in European forms of worship was overcome thanks to the effort of translators. They brought reform from the errors of the old church that ruled Europe for 1260 years as people could now read the Bible directly. The reformists established Churches in the free worlds across the seas in the extended English speaking nations. Primarily the USA became the bastion of religious freedom. Hence we see a Church era that established itself in the general Seventh Day Baptist churches in the USA. That era is still alive and active in the world. Hence the message is for them to "hold fast until I come." This fourth era and subsequent eras all must hold fast till the Last Days.

Summary

Saints, who practice obedience, love, and continual repentance will have the opportunity to guide others toward the salvation they have received, drawing from their own experience. Those who endure the challenges caused by misguided or even malicious leaders are promised rewards for their perseverance in truth and righteousness. While a church may falter in some areas, these messages call for self-examination, guided by God and repentance. Without this, churches risk failing in their mission to lead others to salvation in Jesus Christ. The last four eras, in particular, must remain steadfast in their foundations and uphold the truths they have received until the Messiah returns.

Apocalypse

Chapter 3

More Churches of God

Third Commandment:
"You shall not take the name of Jehovah your God in vain. For Jehovah will not hold him guiltless that takes His name in vain."
(Exodus 20:7, MKJV)

(Worship, loyalty, and obedience cannot exist if there is disrespect for the names of God and Jesus Christ and what they stand for.)

Revelation 3:1-6: Sardis – Fifth Message

"And to the angel of the church in Sardis write: He who has the seven Spirits of God and the seven stars says these things. I know your works, that you have a name that you live, and are dead.
Be watchful and strengthen the things which remain, that are ready to die. For I have not found your works being fulfilled before God. Remember then how you have received and heard, and hold fast, and repent. Therefore if you will not watch, I will come upon you as a

thief, and you will not know what hour I will
come upon you.
You have a few names even in Sardis who
have not defiled their garments. And they will
walk with Me in white, for they are worthy.
The one who overcomes, this one will be
clothed in white clothing. And I will not blot
out his name out of the Book of Life, but I will
confess his name before My Father and before
His angels.
He who has an ear, let him hear what the
Spirit says to the churches."
(Revelation 3:1-6, MKJV)

The church in Sardis appears to have lost its true
faith. Compromise led to the decline of genuine worship,
and most members were influenced by the city's paganism,
failing to guide others away from false worship and sin.

At times, the church as a whole was nearly lost.
However, some individuals remained steadfast amid
widespread paganism and compromise. These members
continued to purify themselves from sin, kept the
Commandments, and refused to defile their lives or
worship. They may still participate in the first resurrection
at Christ's Second Advent.

In recent times, this era has experienced turmoil and
division, partly due to some misguided leadership. Some
have reverted to pagan practices, risking the loss of true
faith and doctrine. They are therefore urged to remain
steadfast until the Last Days.

"Remember then how you have received
and heard, and hold fast, and repent.
Therefore if you will not watch, I will come

upon you as a thief, and you will not know what hour I will come upon you"

In some literature this era seems to be associated with the Seventh Day Adventists which split with the Church of God (Seventh Day) which also split into three groups. Many in the Seventh Days Adventists still hold on to the prophecies of a woman called Ellen White which proved to be false after the failures of 1844. Some elements lean towards the Trinity doctrines and allowing the Eastar festivals of the fertility goddess with her bunny eggs symbols, and even aspects of the sun god. They still hold on to the Sabbath command, but seem to be drifting into paganism in several ways.

Revelation 3:7-13:
Philadelphia – Sixth Message

"And to the angel of the church in Philadelphia write: He who is holy, He who is true, He who has the key of David, He who opens and no one shuts; and shuts and no one opens, says these things:
I know your works. Behold, I have given before you an open door, and no one can shut it. For you have a little strength and have kept My Word and have not denied My name.
Behold, I give out of those of the synagogue of Satan, those saying themselves to be Jews and are not, but lie; behold, I will make them to come and worship before your feet, and to know that I have loved you.

Because you have kept the Word of My
patience, I also will keep you from the hour of
temptation which will come upon all the
habitable world, to try those who dwell upon
the earth.
Behold, I come quickly. Hold fast to that
which you have, so that no one may take your
crown.
Him who overcomes I will make him a pillar in
the temple of My God, and he will go out no
more. And I will write upon him the name of
My God, and the name of the city of My God,
the New Jerusalem, which comes down out of
Heaven from My God, and My new name.
He who has an ear, let him hear what the
Spirit says to the churches."
(Revelation 3:7-13, MKJV)

Philadelphia was a small town, and the authorities of this town allowed Christians to fellowship and evangelise. Apparently there were no big pagan temples nearby, and therefore the church did not suffer great persecution from adherents of pagan temples. Rome probably was not much concerned if the Church of God grew in this town. It did not cause problems for them.

The key of David refers to being the King over Israel. Those in the Church that hold fast to the true worship, and therefore the Covenant to keep the Commandments, can hope to rule with Christ after His return. This was the saying of the prophet.

"And the key of the house of David I will lay
on his shoulder; so he shall open, and none

shall shut; and he shall shut, and none shall open."
(Isaiah 22:22, MKJV)

This was promised to Jesus Christ, the Messiah.

"For David has not ascended into the heavens, but he says himself, "The LORD said to my Lord, Sit at My right hand
until I place Your enemies as a footstool to Your feet."
Therefore let all the house of Israel know assuredly that God made this same Jesus, whom you crucified, both Lord and Christ."
(Acts2:34-36, MKJV)

The open door can also refer to the means and opportunity to preach the Gospel to the general public.

"And, when I came to Troas to preach Christ's gospel, and a door was opened to me by the Lord,"
(2 Corinthians 2:12, MKJV)

This Church had an open door to preach to the town, and they used all the means to do this work. They may have experienced resistance and faced opposition, but those who opposed will one day, on Judgment Day, admit that this Church was right in its doctrine and message. Opposition came mostly from the Jews, as the Gospel was born out of the Jewish faith, and the Jewish priesthood probably would not want to lose membership to the new Faith flourishing in their town.

"And the Scripture, foreseeing that God would justify the nations through faith, preached the gospel before to Abraham, saying, "In you shall all nations be blessed.""
(Galatians 3:8, MKJV)

Jesus was indicating that the opposing Jewish leadership was acting wrong to oppress Christians. At the return of Messiah they will be proven wrong for not becoming Messianic Jews.

The Philadelphia Church could also be seen as an era of the Church at the Last Days. One particular verse stands out in support of this.

"Because you have kept the Word of My patience, I also will keep you from the hour of temptation which will come upon all the habitable world, to try those who dwell upon the earth."
(Revelation 3:10, MKJV)

Some translations refer to "the hour of trial," "testing," or "tribulation." This concept suggests that, in the Last Days, civilizations worldwide will undergo a final test that exposes their faults and failures. This outcome is attributed to humanity's sinfulness and the shortcomings of governments that ignore God's Word and guidance. As a result, their nation-building efforts will be tested and found lacking.

Because of religious freedom in English-speaking nations, God granted them blessings and protection, enabling the Church of God to operate freely and preach the true Gospel.

This period is also known as the Philadelphia era, during which a worldwide Church of God carried out its mission in the name of Jesus Christ. Advances in radio and other communication technologies provided global outreach, which the Church fully utilized to expand internationally. Members are devoted to God and His Commandments, and they avoid pagan practices and festivals.

Members of this Church may be spared from the calamity and great tribulation of the Last Days. Jesus promised that His return is imminent. Those who remain faithful and worship in truth will receive their reward and become eternal residents of the New Jerusalem.

During this era, members and Churches may become scattered but remain committed to the truths they have learned. They have endured apostasy from misguided leaders and have recognized these leaders as false.

"Behold, I give out of those of the synagogue of Satan, those saying themselves to be Jews and are not, but lie; behold, I will make them to come and worship before your feet, and to know that I have loved you."

In the Last Days they will have survived the apostasy to stay true to the original Faith. They may survive the coming tribulation.

Revelation 3:14-22:
Laodicea – Seventh Message

"And to the angel of the church of the
Laodicea write: The Amen, the faithful and
true Witness, the Head of the creation of God,
says these things:
I know your works, that you are neither cold
nor hot. I would that you were cold or hot.
So because you are lukewarm, and neither
cold nor hot, I will vomit you out of My mouth.
Because you say, I am rich and increased
with goods and have need of nothing, and do
not know that you are wretched and
miserable and poor and blind and naked,
I counsel you to buy from Me gold purified by
fire, so that you may be rich; and white
clothing, so that you may be clothed, and so
that the shame of your nakedness does not
appear. And anoint your eyes with eye salve,
so that you may see.
As many as I love, I rebuke and chasten;
therefore be zealous and repent.
Behold, I stand at the door and knock. If
anyone hears My voice and opens the door, I
will come in to him and will dine with him and
he with Me.
 To him who overcomes I will grant to sit with
Me in My throne, even as I also overcame and
have sat down with My Father in His throne.
He who has an ear, let him hear what the
Spirit says to the churches."
(Revelation 3:14-22, MKJV)

Jesus introduced this letter to Laodicea with the confirmation that He is the Amen, the true and faithful Witness, and the Head of the Creation of God. He co-created everything and is head over everything. His testimony is pure and correct.

In the information age, and due to young people's quest for higher education, the population may feel they are enriched with knowledge and don't need Godly knowledge. The Bible is seen as archaic and no longer needed. However, the learned people at the university will find, through their extensive studies in their vast libraries, that prophecies were written about Jesus Christ, that His prophecies were true, and that they will come to pass. Jesus is the final judge, as it was given to him by God the Father. All the arguments and doubts from college professors can and will be shown to have holes in their claims against God and a risen Jesus Christ. If they can face facts and step aside from the state-ordained narrative, they will find Jesus to be the only true Messiah.

This Laodicea church was lukewarm. God was unsure of their loyalty to His Word. They may have sat in Church meetings, but have not done their homework to prove the true worship compared to creeping paganism that can enter worship services. They will not be in the future coming Kingdom of God if they don't fully convert to true Christianity. They will not become saved, having one foot in the sin of the community.

The Church in Laodicea was mostly lost, even though they believed they had entered the eternal Kingdom of God. But Jesus had to break their mold and shake their tree:

"And one said to Him, Lord, are the ones being saved few? And He said to them,

Strive to enter in at the narrow gate. For I say
to you, many will seek to enter in and shall
not be able.
And once the Master of the house has risen
up and has shut the door, and you begin to
stand outside and to knock at the door,
saying, Lord, Lord, open to us, and He shall
answer and say to you, I do not know you;
from where are you;
then you shall begin to say, We ate and drank
in Your presence, and You have taught in our
streets.
But He shall say, I tell you, I do not know you;
from where you are. Depart from Me, all
workers of unrighteousness!
There will be weeping and gnashing of teeth
when you will see Abraham and Isaac and
Jacob, and all the prophets, in the kingdom of
God, and yourselves being thrust out."
(Luke 13:23-28, MKJV)

The city of Laodicea was on a riverbank and at the
crossroads from three directions. Goods would travel by
boat and road to be traded in this city. It was very wealthy,
with a functioning bank, a hospital, and a centre of
education. The people had more than enough money and
were self-sufficient.

This affected the Church, as they acted as if they didn't
really need the guidance and mercy of Jesus Christ. They
seemed to think their existence was assured, and repentance
towards Godly worship was not a priority. Jesus was
concerned about their attitude, leading to a lack of
seriousness in learning the eternal ways of the coming

Kingdom of God. If they did not repent, they would never be in the New Jerusalem!

Jesus admonished them that, spiritually, they are poor and rather worthless. They trust their gold in the bank instead of trusting God. They are blind to their spiritual status, and the hospitals cannot save them forever. They would need to spend much more time and effort in Bible study and in their worship of the Eternal to begin to comprehend their spiritual nakedness and the disease of their spiritual mind.

This church was dead and was not seeking God, nor following Christ to learn the eternal ways that would lead to being granted citizenship in the Jerusalem from above.

Jesus was knocking on the door to be allowed into their goodly homes, to lead them to repentance and a change of heart towards others. They could be rejected in the same way that they were really rejecting Godly obedience.

> "Seek Jehovah while He may be found; call on Him while He is near.
> Let the wicked forsake his way, and the unrighteous man his thoughts; and let him return to Jehovah, and He will have mercy on him; and to our God, for He will abundantly pardon.
> For My thoughts are not your thoughts, nor your ways My ways, says Jehovah.
> For as the heavens are higher than the earth, so are My ways higher than your ways, and My thoughts than your thoughts."
> (Isaiah 55:6-9, MKJV)

If viewed in terms of eras, it may indicate that the Sardis situation exists right in the Last Days before the Second

Advent. Just as Sardis is the last Church on the mail route, so also the Sardis members may have come out of the Philadelphia era. They would be blessed physically but spiritually poor. They may experience the final tribulation. Jesus begged them to rethink their attitude, seek spiritual riches, and learn to trust that He would save them if they studied their Bibles again and sought the true worship of God.

In the Last Days, wars and more rumours of wars will come. Economic collapse will happen as economic sanctions and wars disrupt worldwide trade. Nations will begin to go hungry. Resources will become scarce. Suddenly, the good life is no longer possible. People will be forced to turn to God and Jesus Christ for even physical salvation. The call is to the Church to accept the calamity and to learn to trust God and follow Jesus, in both physical and spiritual salvation. Thus, they must buy from God through prayer and supplication, follow Jesus closely, consider their sinful ways, and grow closer to God through daily repentance, overcoming all temptations in tribulation.

Then they will grow spiritually and later enter the eternal Kingdom of God at the Second Advent, not trusting that their current physical kingdom and riches will last. It cannot save them in the long run. It will disintegrate, as it is not based on God's ways as shown in the Bible.

Evangelism allowed?

The dissemination of God's messages is essential, as the world requires spiritual guidance. Evangelism is necessary to enable individuals in various nations and cities to convert, repent, and pursue righteousness before God. Without such opportunities, there may be no justification to avert catastrophe, conflict, or destruction. Many governments and authorities do not acknowledge God or His Word. While some leaders believe they possess solutions, others recognize their limitations but view leadership as a career pursuit. For certain individuals, political engagement serves as a means to acquire power or wealth through corruption. All such actions are known to God.

If churches are restricted from operating, or if their congregations become unrepentant and cease to grow, there may be no basis for God's mercy to prevent catastrophe.

According to the biblical account, God permitted the destruction of Sodom due to widespread unrighteousness. Abraham interceded on behalf of the city, seeking its preservation for a few righteous individuals who worshipped and obeyed God and upheld His commandments.

"Far be it from You to act in this manner, to kill the righteous with the wicked. And far be it from You, that the righteous should be as the wicked. Shall not the Judge of all the earth do right?
And Jehovah said, If I find in Sodom fifty righteous within the city, then I will spare all the place for their sakes."
(Genesis 18:25-26, MKJV)

Ultimately Abraham argued to spare Sodom for the sake of just ten righteous people.

"And he said, Oh do not let Jehovah be angry, and I will speak only once more. Perhaps ten

shall be found there. And He said, I will not destroy it for ten's sake.
And Jehovah went His way as soon as He had left off talking with Abraham. And Abraham returned to his place."
(Genesis 18:32-33, MKJV)

According to Genesis 19, Lot and his family did not conform to the prevailing social and political pressures in Sodom. The narrative describes how angels visited Lot and how the citizens of Sodom sought to impose their desires on them. As a result, Lot and his family were instructed to leave, and Sodom was subsequently destroyed.

The continued presence of Churches and the ongoing conversion and repentance of individuals are presented as factors that may prevent apocalyptic events.

Therefore, these messages are directed toward religious communities and policymakers, emphasizing the importance of religious freedom, evangelism, and encouraging repentance and worship to avert apocalyptic outcomes.

Summary

Governments must allow Christian evangelizing. However, preventing evangelizing will allow the forces of evil to overcome the civilized behaviour of societies.

Churches of God must also evangelize and grow in size and quality of converts. The Apocalypse may come if the Church fails in purity of faith and practice. People may experience apocalyptic events if no Church practices the true faith, or if they are prevented by governments from practicing the true religion.

Chapter 4

God Revealed

Fourth Commandment:
"Remember the Sabbath day, to keep it holy.
Six days you shall labor and do all your work.
But the seventh day is the Sabbath of Jehovah your
God. You shall not do any work, you, nor your son,
nor your daughter, your manservant, nor your
maidservant, nor your cattle, nor your stranger
within your gates.
For in six days Jehovah made the heavens and the
earth, the sea, and all that is in them, and rested
the seventh day. Therefore Jehovah blessed the
Sabbath day, and sanctified it."
(Exodus 20:8-11, MKJV)

(The Most High God is identified by His defined
sacred times. By worshipping on Biblical days,
we show that we accept His authority over our
lives.)

After the messages to the Churches of God a vision of the throne of God is provided. It is wise to consider every verse in detail.

"After these things I looked, and behold, a door was opened in Heaven. And the first

voice which I heard was as it were of a
trumpet talking with me, saying, Come up
here, and I will show you what must occur
after these things."
(Revelation 4:1, MKJV)

The voice that sounded like a trumpet blowing in full strength was that of the Lamb. It was Jesus the Christ, who is at the right hand at God's throne. He suffered because of the sinful human condition but stayed pure and was accepted as out High Priest forever. He was granted to raise the Churches of God.

After the Churches of God in gentile nations were established through Paul, they were supported by other Apostles and were under authorship of Church rule from Jerusalem. This was the case at that time before Jerusalem was destroyed. The growing sum of the saints will be filled over 2 millenniums, but humankind's governments who act as though God does not exist will fail and fail again, leading to endless wars. This is what would happen after the establishment and spread of the Churches of God throughout the world.

"And immediately I became in spirit. And
behold, a throne was set in Heaven, and One
sat upon the throne."
(Revelation 4:2, MKJV)

God Almighty, the Father of Jesus Christ, the One by who's Will the universe and humankind were created, is now described. By His Will Jesus ordered the universe to be formed by the Angels of God. Almighty God, the Father of Jesus Christ, will now be shown on His throne in Heaven.

> "And He who sat there looked like a jasper stone and a sardius. And a rainbow was around the throne, looking like an emerald." (Revelation 4:3, MKJV)

Jasper is usually green, and sardius is green. God is not seen directly, but is surrounded by a multi-coloured rainbow cloud predominantly lit by the light from the Throne shining through and coloured by these crystals. Emerald has the capability to fracture light into many different coloured beams.

> "And around the throne I saw twenty-four thrones. And on the thrones I saw twenty-four elders sitting, clothed in white clothing. And they had crowns of gold on their heads." (Revelation 4:4, MKJV)

These figures are considered highly senior angels. Their white garments symbolize purity before God. Consequently, they have been granted authority within their respective spheres of influence, as signified by their golden crowns. They preside over the twelve tribes of Israel and may currently serve a dual role in maintaining the separation of church and state. Additionally, they guided the twelve apostles, who are expected to govern Israel's twelve tribes when church and state are reunited upon the return of the Messiah.

"and made us kings **and** priests to God and
His Father, to Him be glory and dominion
forever and ever. Amen."
(Revelation 1:6, MKJV) [Emphasis mine]

This was promised to the apostles, as they were
made perfect and 100% trustworthy through their
sufferings as they follow Jesus.

"And out of the throne came lightnings and
thunderings and voices. And seven lamps of
fire were burning in front of the throne, which
are the seven spirits of God."
(Revelation 4:5, MKJV)

The seven lamps represent the seven spirits that
Jesus controls and sent out to the seven Churches of God,
as seen in Chapter 1:13.

"And a sea of glass was in front of the throne,
like crystal. And in the midst of the throne,
and around the throne, were four living
creatures, full of eyes in front and behind."
(Revelation 4:6, MKJV)

The crystal could indicate the need for transparency
when appearing before the Throne of God. Then four
creatures are shown. It is possible that these beings appear
before God as representatives of God's creation. Four
beings representing creatures on the earth are named, and
they form the most important animal in each group.

"The first living creature was like a lion, the
second living creature was like an ox, the

third living creature had a face like a human, and the fourth living creature was like a flying eagle."
(Revelation 4:7, MKJV)

A lion is the pinnacle of the wild animals. The ox is the pinnacle of the domesticated animals, used for ploughing. The human is unique and the master of all the animals. The eagle is the most majestic of the birds. These all seems to indicate that God created all, and is the master of them all. The creation on the earth existed at His command, and honours God.

"Each of the four living creatures had six wings and were full of eyes inside and out. Without stopping day or night they were saying, "Holy, holy, holy is the Lord God Almighty, who was, who is, and who is coming.""
(Revelation 4:8, MKJV)

In early Biblical history we find indications that God was on the earth directing His creation. God walked in the Garden of Eden, before Adam and Eve sinned, and was banished from the garden. God also seems to have left the garden and it was neglected. But we can see in Revelation and other scriptures that God will eventually return to the earth in all His Glory and exist in the New Jerusalem. So the Lord God Almighty was, and still is on His throne, and is coming to Jerusalem after Jesus Christ have reigned for a thousand years.

"Then the end will come, when after he has done away with every ruler and every

authority and power, the Messiah hands over
the kingdom to God the Father."
(1 Corinthians 15:24, MKJV)

The 24 Elders are Angels that are ruling over the
earth under God's command. They see what is happening
in the creation and gives glory to God for having creating it
all.

"Whenever the living creatures give glory,
honor, and thanks to the one who sits on the
throne, who lives forever and ever,
the 24 elders bow down and worship in front
of the one who sits on the throne, the one who
lives forever and ever. They throw their
victor's crowns in front of the throne and say,
"You are worthy, our Lord and God, to receive
glory, honor, and power, because you created
all things; they came into existence and were
created because of your will.""
(Revelation 4:9-11, MKJV)

Chapter 5

Jesus Christ Revealed

Fifth Commandment:
"Honor your father and your mother, so that your days may be long upon the land which Jehovah your God gives you."
(Exodus 20:12, MKJV)

(Jesus honored His heavenly Father, showing how we must honor our parents; otherwise, we will go astray and cause conflict, and be in danger of becoming outcasts.)

Someone had to be able to walk perfectly before God as a flesh and blood human being on the earth. Someone had to be worthy of judging humankind. Someone had to prove that righteousness is possible among humans. Someone had to overcome evil. Else God will simply allow the world to sink into anarchy and self-destruct. Humankind would go the way of the dinosaurs.

Someone lived a complete righteous life in the face of persecution. Someone has the right to judge between fake and truth, between evil and good, between the righteous and sinners. Such a being did walk the earth, and is qualified to be Messiah and judge. After His achievement, humanity has no excuse anymore.

The book of Revelation now describes Jesus the Christ, who perfectly honored His heavenly Father.

During this historical period, the practice of writing a book involved rolling a long piece of paper or specially prepared leather and placing it inside a vase. As the material was rolled, a seal was affixed to each side. The presence of seven seals signified a covenant, specifically with the saints who were persecuted for adhering to the Commandments and proclaiming the Gospel of Jesus Christ. Despite efforts by the ruling elite and broader society to suppress the saints and eradicate the Gospel, the opposite effect occurred. The number of saints increased, the Gospel continued to spread, and more individuals observed the Commandments that others had neglected. Ultimately, it is asserted that God will hold the elite rulers and unjust legal systems accountable for their wrongful persecution of the saints.

As a set of seals is broken, a section of the scroll is revealed and its writing can be read and executed.

Revelation 5:1-3

"And I saw a book on the right of Him sitting on the throne, written inside and on the back, sealed with seven seals.
And I saw a mighty angel proclaiming with a loud voice, Who is worthy to open the book and to loosen its seals?
And no one in Heaven, nor on the earth, nor under the earth, was able to open the book or to look at it."
(Revelation 5:1-3, MKJV)

There are three categories of intelligent beings.

There are those currently in Heaven. They are the Angels, Archangels, Elders and other beings around the Throne of God.

Secondly there are human beings alive on the earth. A few are honouring God and obeying Him as far as they can possibly do with their limited capabilities.

Thirdly some have died and are in graves or Hades as it is sometimes labelled in the Bible. They can be resurrected, but so far only Jesus Christ was resurrected and is alive today. The rest will be resurrected in future events, as we will see later. However, none are worthy to allow the scroll to be opened and the sequences to continue.

Revelation 5:4-5

"And I wept very much, because no one was found worthy to open and to read the book, nor to look at it.
And one of the elders said to me, Do not weep. Behold, the Lion of the tribe of Judah, the Root of David, has prevailed to open the book and to loose the seven seals of it."
(Revelation 5:4-5, MKJV)

The world crucified the Son of God. The world is still denying and crucifying the Son of God in their minds today. Some Hollywood idols are teaching the world the violent ways of Satan, and to blaspheme the name of the Son of God. Billions happily learn the evil ways and disrespect towards Jesus Christ, and so spiritually crucify Him daily. There are even religions that teach billions of people to deny that Jesus is the Christ, the Son of God.

"Beloved, do not believe every spirit, but try
the spirits to see if they are of God, because
many false prophets have gone out into the
world.
By this you know the Spirit of God: every
spirit that confesses that Jesus Christ has
come in the flesh is of God;
and every spirit that does not confess that
Jesus Christ has come in the flesh is not of
God. And this is the antichrist you heard is
coming, and even now is already in the
world."
(1 John 4:1-3, MKJV)

This same Son of God proved His enduring love of
God, and love for humans, even unto death.

Jesus the Christ is worthy and justified to open the
scrolls of the apocalypse. Those that followed Him and was
vilified by the world must receive the promises made to the
patriarchs of salvation and inheritance.

Jesus already received some of the promises of
God. This is described in this chapter.

Revelation 5:6-9

"And I looked, and lo, in the midst of the
throne and of the four living creatures, amidst
the elders, a Lamb stood, as if it had been
slain, having seven horns and seven eyes,
which are the seven Spirits of God sent forth
into all the earth.

And He came and took the book out of the right hand of Him sitting on the throne.
And when He had taken the book, the four living creatures and the twenty-four elders fell down before the Lamb, each one having harps and golden vials full of incense, which are the prayers of the saints.
And they sang a new song, saying, You are worthy to take the book and to open its seals, for You were slain and have redeemed us to God by Your blood out of every kindred and tongue and people and nation.
And You made us kings and priests to our God, and we will reign over the earth."
(Revelation 5:6-9, MKJV)

The 24 elders relates to those over the twelve tribes of Israel. Currently there is a separation between Church and State, which was allowed when Israel wanted a King as well to compliment the prophet and priests. From that time a duel system of rule existed, hence twenty four Elders in Heaven, showing the duel system. The song is the worship of not only saints of the twelve tribes of Israel, but also saints from other nations around the world. They worship God in prayers every day, following Messiah in His Faith and obedience.

When Messiah returns, the resurrected saints from around the world will become fully developed to unite the roles of Priests and Kings again, as God wanted it to be from the beginning.

"And I looked, and I heard the voice of many angels around the throne, and the living creatures and the elders. And the number of

them was myriads and myriads, and
thousands of thousands,
saying with a great voice, Worthy is the Lamb
who was slain, to receive power and riches
and wisdom and strength and honor and glory
and blessing.
And I heard every creature which is in the
Heaven and on the earth, and under the
earth, and those that are in the sea, and all
who are in them, saying, Blessing and honor
and glory and power be to Him sitting on the
throne, and to the Lamb forever and ever.
And the four living creatures said, Amen. And
the twenty-four elders fell down and
worshiped the One living forever and ever."
(Revelation 5:6-14, MKJV)

Summary

Salvation was and still is made possible through the
sacrifice and saving work of Jesus Christ, our High Priest.
He intercedes for us before the throne of God. He proved
total loyalty and righteousness before God. He is, therefore,
fully worthy of the worship by humanity and Angels in
Heaven. Without the saving grace and action of Jesus
Christ, a permanent solution to the problems of sin and
corruption of humanity would not be possible. The
wonderful creation work of God in humanity would all go
to waste. Without the salvation brought by Jesus Christ, the
final apocalypse will ruin everything, and there will be no
escape from utter destruction. Jesus is worthy of complete
adoration and worship as our eternal High Priest in Heaven.

Chapter 6

Seals Unsealed

Sixth Commandment:
"You shall not kill."
(Exodus 20:13, MKJV)

(God values life! He does not want to see any killing. But due to sin, humanity became cut off from God's life, even eternal life. The result is that humankind justifies all the killing we see.)

The world would develop towards economic interdependence. That brings the danger of sanctions, economic depression, hunger, disease, pandemics, and wars. It even brings the possibility of world wars.

God's ways and laws bring economic freedom and protection. The Bible shows the Jubilee system, but will the rich allow that? Not even in the Promised Land was it allowed by the rich and elite.

The failure to seriously consider God's guidance triggers the first 4 seals. The four horsemen of the apocalypse are already running, and increasing in worldwide disasters.

Firstly, we see manmade religions and leaders. These religious leaders go out to gain followers and worshippers by force. They can even use the police and military to force people to worship their idea of a god or gods. Often, those who refuse are persecuted, jailed, and even killed. Be aware that dictators in the world also set themselves up as religious-type leaders that must be worshipped, often by force. In true Godly worship, freedom of worship exists. Members are evangelised, but not forced by military means. However, the nature of the rider of the first horse is to use force to enforce his particular idea of religion. He has the bow in his hand to kill opponents.

Different leaders of different nations formed different man-made religions, creating the potential for conflict, war, famine, and disease.

Revelation 6:1-8

"And I saw when the Lamb opened one of the seals, and I heard one of the four living creatures like a sound of thunder, saying, Come and see.
And I saw. And behold a white horse! And he sitting on it had a bow. And a crown was given to him, and he went forth conquering and to conquer.
And when He had opened the second seal, I heard the second living creature say, Come and see.
And another, a red horse, went out. And power was given to him sitting on it, to take peace from the earth, and that they should kill one another. And there was given to him a great sword.
And when He had opened the third seal, I heard the third living creature say, Come and see. And I looked, and lo, a black horse. And he sitting on it had a balance in his hand.

And I heard a voice in the midst of the four living creatures say, A choenix of wheat for a denarius, and three choenixes of barley for a denarius. And do not hurt the oil and the wine.
And when He had opened the fourth seal, I heard the voice of the fourth living creature say, Come and see.
And I looked, and behold, a pale horse. And the name of him sitting on it was Death, and Hell followed with him. And authority was given to them over the fourth part of the earth, to kill with the sword and with hunger and with death and by the beasts of the earth."
(Revelation 6:1-8, MKJV)

WW1 and WW2 have already demonstrated these evils. The cycle continues. WW3 will be the worst, as the name of Jesus Christ is blasphemed on the media by idols, and His guidance and Commandments are disrespected. His rule and sceptre is belittled. It started in Jerusalem when Jews and Gentiles rejected Jesus Christ, and had Him crucified.

"Son of man, prophesy and say, So says Jehovah. Say, A sword, a sword is sharpened and also polished.
It is sharpened in order to slaughter; it is polished so that there may be a flash to it. Or shall we rejoice? You are despising the **rod of My son**, as if it were every tree.
And He has given it to be polished, to be taken by the hand. The sword, it is sharpened, and

it it polished, to give it into the hand of the
slayer.
Cry and howl, son of man; for it shall be on
My people; it shall be on all the rulers of
Israel. They are thrown to the sword with My
people; Therefore slap your thigh.
Because it is a trial, and what if even the
despising rod shall not be? says the Lord
Jehovah.
And you, son of man, prophesy and strike
your hands together; and let **the sword be
doubled the third time**, the sword of the
slain. It is the sword of the slain, the great one
that surrounds them;"
(Ezekiel 21:9-14, MKJV) [Emphasis mine]

As the blasphemy and disregard continues in the
world, some people respond to the preaching of evangelists,
and convert, and repent. They are made righteous. A grace
period will be allowed till the number for the first
resurrection at the Second Advent is sealed. The rest of the
world will be heading into WW3.

Revelation 6:9-11

"And when He had opened the fifth seal, I saw
under the altar the souls of those who had
been slain for the Word of God, and for the
testimony which they held.
And they cried with a loud voice, saying, Until
when, Master, holy and true, do You not judge
and avenge our blood on those who dwell on
the earth?

And white robes were given to each one of
them. And it was said to them that they
should rest yet for a little time, until both
their fellow servants and their brothers (those
about to be killed as they were) should have
their number made complete."
(Revelation 6:9-11, MKJV)

After this grace period, and the number of saints is
completed, the apocalypse can continue, since the rest of
humanity will not repent unless they face a tribulation.
Those who died having kept the Faith are granted white
robes, indicating their ratification of the Covenant that
promised them a place in the first resurrection at the
Second Advent of the Messiah, when He will begin to reign
from Jerusalem.

The writings of the sixth seal indicate an environmental
disaster in the near future.

A super volcano will blast again as before. It will spew
dust into the upper atmosphere. This will circle the earth
and cause a climate catastrophe. Crops will fail, and hunger
will spread. Add to that the massive pollution caused by
wars, and the perfect storm for a worldwide ecological
disaster develops.

Revelation 6:12-17

"And when He had opened the sixth seal, I
looked, and behold, there was a great
earthquake. And the sun became black as
sackcloth of hair, and the moon became like
blood.

And the stars of heaven fell to the earth, even
as a fig tree casts her untimely figs when she
is shaken by a mighty wind.
And the heaven departed like a scroll when it
is rolled together. And every mountain and
island were moved out of their places.
And the kings of the earth, and the great men,
and the rich, and the chief captains, and the
mighty men, and every bondman, and every
freeman, hid themselves in the dens and in
the rocks of the mountains.
And they said to the mountains and rocks,
Fall on us and hide us from the face of Him
sitting on the throne, and from the wrath of
the Lamb;
for the great day of His wrath has come, and
who will be able to stand?"
(Revelation 6:12-17, MKJV)

Summary

Mountains in the Bible often refer to the seat of
kingdoms. Cities were usually built on hills so that
approaching enemies could be seen from far away, and
gates were closed to defend against attacking armies. When
the world is at war, even gated communities and walled
cities will not save anyone. Governments can be moved and
cease to exist.

When the balance of powers between nations is
shaken, treaties on scrolls are ignored. It is as if the safe
haven of international courts is shaken, and scrolls rolled
back as if they did not exist.

Apocalypse

The continual destruction of war leaves a cloud of smoke that casts a shadow over civilizations. The sun and moon become obscured.

Kings and senior politicians run to their bunkers or caves. The elite go into hiding from the war and destruction. They eradicated and banned Christianity from schools and the justice system. Symbols of the Ten Commandments were removed from courts. Hence, the elite knew that they opposed the Messiah and His Law. There is no point in praying for forgiveness. The only plan they have is to hide from the approaching wrath.

This is the result of persecuting Christian leaders and banning evangelizing for Christ. This justifies the unsealing of Apocalypse by Messiah.

Apocalypse

Chapter 7

Sealing the Saints

Seventh Commandment:
"You shall not commit adultery."
(Exodus 20:14, MKJV)

(The biggest mistake the Churches can make is to commit adultery, physically and spiritually, thereby allowing pollution of body and mind, which cause disease to wreak havoc in their midst.)

Some churches are allowing gay priests and gay marriages. They violate the Commandment directly and physically. None of their members can claim to be saints. Spiritual adultery or fornication refers to incorporation of aspects of other religious systems and even atheism or paganism into Christian worship. None of such membership can claim to be saints.

Firstly, from the twelve tribes of Israel dispersed throughout the world, a 144,000 repented from rejecting Jesus as the Christ and Messiah. They have proven the true Gospel and have repented. They have made the New Covenant and have kept the Commandments. If ever they fall, they repented and restored their faith and walk with God. They are sealed as they face a loss of life but refuse to reject Jesus as the Christ. They see and follow Him as the final prophet that kept the Law even as He faced the crucifixion. They follow in His footsteps.

This is evident from Revelation 7:1-8

Revelation 7:1-8

"And after these things I saw four angels
standing on the four corners of the earth,
holding the four winds of the earth so that the
wind should not blow on the earth, nor on the
sea, nor on any tree.
And I saw another angel ascending from the
east, having the seal of the living God. And he
cried with a loud voice to the four angels, to
whom it was given to hurt the earth and the
sea,
saying, Do not hurt the earth or the sea or the
trees until we have sealed the servants of our
God in their foreheads.
And I heard the number of those who were
sealed, one hundred and forty-four
thousands, having been sealed out of every
tribe of the sons of Israel."
(Revelation 7:1-4, MKJV)

In this list of tribes from which the 144,000 through
the great tribulation would come is a variance from the
initial list of twelve tribes stemming from the patriarchs.
This needs to be explained here:

In the list that follows in Revelation 7:4-9, it is
noted that **Dan is left out, and replaced by Manasseh,**
probably due to excessive sin. It seems that from the
beginning Dan was a problem for Jacob, the patriarch, from
whom the twelve sons came that formed the twelve tribes

of Israel. Dan was the son of the slave woman, Jacob's other wife, and was quite judgmental of the other sons of Rachel, wife of Jacob. This was evident and prophesied to become a big problem in Israel.

"Dan shall judge his people, as one of the tribes of Israel.
Dan shall be a serpent by the way, an adder in the path, that bites the horse's heels, so that its rider shall fall backward."
(Genesis 49:16-17, MKJV)

The tribe of Dan seemed to be a problem for God, in that they criticize the other tribes and their attempts at worshipping God. This tribe easily worshipped pagan images, and so left the true faith for paganism. Therefor another half tribe, Manasseh, was told to keep them from completely falling away.

"And the sons of **Dan** set up the engraved image. And Jonathan, the son of Gershom, the son of **Manasseh**, he and his sons were priests to the tribe of Dan until the day of the captivity of the land."
(Judges 18:30, MKJV) [Emphasis mine]

The wayward acts of Dan misled some Israelites and caused a falling away. See 1 Kings 12:28-31. Ultimately Dan was completely rejected for setting up an alternative religion in Samaria that misled the northern tribes of Israel.

"They who swear by the sin of Samaria
and say, As your god lives, O Dan; and,
As the way of Beer-sheba lives; even
they shall fall and never rise up again."
(Amos 8:14, MKJV)

The tribe of Dan was forever rejected and lost their heritage. As a tribe, they were replaced in the heritage list by the family of a son of another tribe.

The twelve tribes of Israel developed from the twelve sons Jacob. One of the twelve tribes was from Joseph, and he had two sons, who were grandsons from Jacob. With Dan falling away, God allowed the family of a grandson to replace Dan. God allowed Manasseh, son of Joseph, grandson of Jacob, to become one of the twelve tribes of Israel, replacing Dan. Let's look at the sons of Joseph, grandsons of Jacob:

"And Joseph called the name of the
first-born Manasseh, saying, For God
has made me forget all my toil and all
my father's house.
And the name of the second he called
Ephraim, saying, For God has caused
me to be fruitful in the land of my
affliction."
(Genesis 41:51-52, MKJV)

So the tribe of Joseph continued, and a section of it was separated and replaced Dan. Therefor the twelve tribes of Israel are still complete in the New Testament, with Dan being rejected and Manasseh taking over. Hence in the salvation picture of the promised Messiah, Dan was replaced by Manasseh. Dan set up a pagan religion in the northern section of the land of Israel, in the province of Samaria. They opposed the true worship in Jerusalem, and lost salvation and eventually inheritance.

When Jesus walked the earth in the Promised Land, He visited Samaria to provide salvation to those living in that area, but few repented and even less stayed in the Faith. Manasseh was one of the two sons of Joseph, and therefore a half tribe of the second order. When it comes to salvation through Christ, God replaced Dan with Manasseh. God is not mocked! Dan paid a high price!

After those from the new list of the twelve tribes of Israel are sealed through their trials in the great tribulation, a second group is also sealed in the same tribulation. From the rest of the world's society a great multitude also make a covenant to keep the Commandments of God forever. They are sealed as they keep the true Faith of Jesus Christ and assist in spreading the Gospel even when facing tribulation and persecution for their Faith.

Revelation 7:9-14

"After these things I looked, and lo, a great multitude, which no man could number, out of all nations and kindreds and people and tongues, stood before the throne and before

the Lamb, clothed with white robes, with
palms in their hands."
(Revelation 7:9, MKJV)

These are sealed as they live into the great
tribulation. Other saints have been sealed before the great
tribulation, but these are the ones that are sealed as they
experience the great calamity on the earth. They keep the
Faith and Commandments, as they suffered in a world that
is being ruined around them.

"And one of the elders answered, saying to
me, Who are these who are arrayed in white
robes, and from where do they come?
And I said to him, Sir, you know. And he said
to me, These are the ones who came out of the
great tribulation and have washed their robes,
and have whitened them in the blood of the
Lamb."
(Revelation 7:13-14, MKJV)

Summary

Some Christians who are not fully committed may respond
positively during the coming great tribulation. They will
need to draw closer to God and Jesus Christ, learning
wisdom and living in a way that reflects their faith.
Otherwise, they risk falling into unchristian behavior and
facing the dangers of a world at war. This is not a time to
be undecided. It is a moment to make choices and face the
results. God wants to know where each person stands. This
is the time when the saints are being sealed.

Chapter 8

The Seventh Seal

Eight Commandment:
"You shall not steal."
(Exodus 20:15, MKJV)

(A big problem with world governments and large industries is the prevalence of corporate greed, leading to lobbying and corruption of governments. Resources are being ruthlessly exploited and stolen from poor inhabitants. The theft leads to people ultimately taking up arms to fight for survival and ultimate equality.)

The seventh seal provides great detail as to the Last Days before Messiah will be sent to prevent the final annihilation and extinction of humans.

The events that will follow are quite terrible. Humans are bringing this on themselves by their own actions and their disregard for the wisdom from God. The Eternal will not intervene to hold back on the calamity that will befall the whole earth. He wants to see people learn from Him and develop into sons and daughters of God, so that they can gain salvation and eternal life through Jesus Christ. When that is not possible due to the unchristian ways and teachings together with persecution of evangelists and pastors, the end of the godless leadership can come. Mistakes made will have such devastating consequences that there was silence in Heaven as the Angels of God anticipated the horrors that will soon befall humankind.

Revelation 8:1-13

"And when He opened the seventh seal, there was silence in Heaven for about half an hour." (Revelation 8:1, MKJV)

Now it is revealed that seven Angels will declare the ways in which societies will fail. They have seen humanity fail before in many ways. After the biggest failure leading to the crucifixion, they can clearly show what the future holds in the absence of Godly guidance.

Injustices are done to peaceful Christians. This leads to the desperate prayers for God to intervene. These prayers will come up before God, and there will be repercussions. Ungodly people will not get away with their sin and crime.

"And I saw the seven angels who stood before God, and seven trumpets were given to them. And another angel came and stood at the altar, having a golden censer. And many incenses were given to him, so that he should offer it with the prayers of all saints on the golden altar before the throne.
And the smoke of the incense which came with the prayers of the saints, ascended up before God from the angel's hand." (Revelation 8:2-4, MKJV)

Societies where Christians are oppressed will fail. There are consequences for unfair and lawless treatment of people under oppressive regimes. When justice fails, God takes notice, and it all gets added to convict the failing governments who don't act against all the oppression that people suffer.

"And the angel took the censer and filled it with fire from the altar, and cast it into the earth. And voices and thunderings and lightnings and an earthquake occurred." (Revelation 8:5, MKJV)

This expresses God's displeasure of the failures of governments, leaders, and of corruption and pollutions of the earth by industry leaders, and in particular mistreatment of Christians, and prevention of the Gospel.

"And the seven angels which had the seven trumpets prepared themselves to sound." (Revelation 8:6, MKJV)

What follows is a classic description of the results of wars. It is described as though a meteor entered our solar system and fell on the earth.

At first the carbon ice melts and is blown away by the solar wind. This exposes the lose boulders, rocks and sand. Gravity from the earth pulls it apart as it nears our planet. One by one several sections hit the atmosphere and it burns as it hits the planet. This is one explanation.

However, this section also describes wars and the result of wars. It is as if hell fell from the sky and destroyed cities, suburbs, industrial complexes and infrastructures. Missiles and drones rain from the sky as if burning hail falls out of heaven.

"The first angel sounded, and there followed
hail and fire mixed with blood, and they were
cast on the earth. And the third part of trees
was burned up, and all green grass was
burned up."
(Revelation 8:7, MKJV)

Conventional wars have a terrible effect on the
environment. Forests are damaged by incessant shelling.
Grasslands are blown to pieces by shells, missiles and
drones. Farmlands catch fire and produce are burnt:

"And the second angel sounded, and as it
were a great mountain burning with fire was
cast into the sea. And the third part of the sea
became blood.
And the third part of the creatures in the sea,
those having souls, died; and the third part of
the ships was destroyed."
(Revelation 8:8-9, MKJV)

As a prelude, a meteor may burn as it enters the
atmosphere. This may be a sign in the sky.
However, the wars on land will expand to the seas.
Ships carrying produce are damaged and destroyed. They
spill pollution into the sea, causing damage to marine
ecosystems. This has long term repercussions as fish
becomes polluted and nations lose a great source of meat. It
leads to death of creatures and people.

"And the third angel sounded, and a great star
burning like a lamp fell from the heaven, and

it fell on the third part of the rivers and on the
fountains of waters.
And the name of the star is called Wormwood,
and a third part of the waters became
wormwood. And many men died from the
waters, because they were made bitter."
(Revelation 8:10-11, MKJV)

War machines cross rivers, getting blown up in
those rivers. Pollutants enter the river systems harming
more fish and ecosystems in those rivers. The dust from all
the rockets, missiles and shells exploding cast a shadow
over the land. It is as if the sun becomes blocked from
shining on land, suburbs and cities.

"And the fourth angel sounded, and the third
part of the sun was stricken, and the third
part of the moon, and the third part of the
stars, so that the third part of them was
darkened, and the day did not appear for a
third part of it, and the night also."
(Revelation 8:12, MKJV)

As a result the world will experience crop failures.
Nations will scramble for food. Governments will prepare
for more wars. A terrible time will lie ahead.

"And I saw and I heard one angel flying in
mid-heaven, saying with a loud voice, Woe!
Woe! Woe to the inhabitants of the earth, from
the rest of the voices of the trumpet of the
three angels being about to sound!"
(Revelation 8:13, MKJV)

A continual cycle of confrontations and wars lies ahead. The four horsemen of false religions, wars, hunger and death will run throughout the world. We may call it sectarianism, military operations, food inflation and collapsing health services. The cycle is the same, and gets worse as it comes around time after time.

Summary

When the seventh seal is broken, it reveals the final wars of humanity. It reveals the blowing of trumpets. Trumpets were used to order troops on the battlefield. Hence, the blowing of trumpets by the Angels shows wars and the consequences of those wars.

Chapter 9

The Fifth Angel and First Woe

Ninth Commandment:
"You shall not bear false witness against your neighbor."
(Exodus 20:16, MKJV)

(Governments will justify the wars they cause. Fake news will justify the destruction. The failure to honestly assess international relationships leads to misinformation and confrontations.)

A brief summary of the reasons for upcoming global calamities and atrocities is provided below.

God sent His Son to demonstrate how a true child of God should live, exemplifying worship, honesty, compassion, and all positive attributes of character and spirit. He fully embodied the Spirit of God and obeyed His Commandments and Law. Despite this, humanity rejected and killed Him. Today, through actions, thoughts, and societal systems, humanity continues to reject Jesus Christ. Although God has sent apostles and is preparing disciples, people persist in sin and continue to persecute pastors and evangelists.

Another possibility is that God allowed a meteor and its debris to enter the atmosphere to remind humanity of its mortality and temporary existence. Civilizations that persisted in worshipping false gods were previously allowed to fall, and some life forms were permitted to become extinct. Today, the Bible is widely available, yet many do not engage with its teachings or seek God's wisdom and guidance. If people continue to view life as accidental and adhere to state religions, God may allow events to proceed without intervention.

And so the first Woe will happen. When famine strikes, humanity turns to war. Chapter 9 of Revelation describes the vision that the Apostle John had of modern world wars.

Revelation 9:1-21

"And the fifth angel sounded. And I saw a star fall from the heaven to the earth, and it was given the key of the abyss.
And it opened the bottomless pit. And there arose a smoke out of the pit, like the smoke of a great furnace. And the sun and air were darkened because of the smoke of the pit."
(Revelation 9:1-2, MKJV)

Most people in the world have seen images of intercontinental missiles rise from their underground silos. What is not generally known is the amount of war machines that have been hidden in bunkers, silos and disused mines. There are a lot of armaments hidden from view. They will arise out of the abyss to make war.

"And out of the smoke came forth locusts onto the earth. And authority was given to them, as the scorpions of the earth have authority.
And they were commanded not to hurt the grass of the earth, or any green thing, or any tree, but only those men who do not have the seal of God in their foreheads."
(Revelation 9:3-4, MKJV)

The images of helicopters and similar vehicles that can rise out of their hidden places are clear. Even some of their missiles have been aptly named 'Stinger missiles'. A new trend is to arm them with chemical and biological weapons, so that people with specifically indoctrinated state ideologies can be killed, but infrastructure and food supplies can be saved. Mostly soldiers will be killed. True Christians may refuse to kill in the name of state religions and ideologies. Some biological weapons will just incapacitate people, so that the enemies can take over and control countries and prepare to capture and reindoctrinate the people to accept the enemies' ideology. The narrative may also indicate that the war machines provide precision strike capabilities to destroy infrastructure and soldiers, but not food production and storage places.

> "And to them it was given that they should not kill them, but that they should be tormented five months. And their torment was like a scorpion's torment when he stings a man.
> And in those days men will seek death and will not find it. And they will long to die, and death will flee from them."
> (Revelation 9:5-6, MKJV)

Such will be the fate of incapacitated soldiers and their families due to chemical weapons. Biological warfare will make them lame, and they can then easily be captured. They will know that the good life they had is forever gone, and oppression and poverty will come. A terribly sad future will await people. It will be significant to see a particular war around Jerusalem that lasts five months. Revelation continues to describe the imagery of their warfare.

> "And the shapes of the locusts were like horses prepared for battle. And on their heads were as it were crowns like gold, and their faces were like the faces of men.
> And they had hairs like the hairs of women, and their teeth were like the teeth of lions.
> And they had breastplates like breastplates of iron. And the sound of their wings was like the sound of chariots of many horses running to battle.
> And they had tails like scorpions, and there were stings in their tails. And their authority was to hurt men five months.
> And they had a king over them, the angel of the bottomless pit, whose name in the Hebrew tongue is Abaddon, but in Greek his name is Apollyon."
> (Revelation 9:7-11, MKJV)

The name here refers to a place of the dead and also the spiritual leader and deputies whose influence and indoctrination lead to death. Satan is consigned to ultimate elimination, and the name ultimately refers to Satan. His rebellion against God leads to the misuse of God's creation and the ultimate wastage of the civilisations built without God's clear guidance, Commandments, Law, and worship.

> "The first woe is past. Behold, after these things yet come two woes."
> (Revelation 9:12, MKJV)

Apocalypse

Whereas the first Woe describes "wars and rumours of war", the second Woe describes a full world war. Missile technology and rapid international travel of war machines mean that a world war can rapidly escalate to a full-on world war that explodes within a year to wreak devastation over the whole world. Current advances in hypersonic missiles can even shorten that period of worldwide devastation to one hour.

"And the sixth angel sounded his trumpet.
And I heard a voice from the four horns of the golden altar before God,
saying to the sixth angel who had the trumpet, Loose the four angels who are bound at the great river Euphrates.
And the four angels were loosed, who were prepared for an hour, and a day, and a month, and a year, in order to slay the third part of men.
And the number of the armies of the horsemen was two myriads of myriads. And I heard their number.
And so I saw the horses in the vision, and those sitting on them, having breastplates of fire, even dusky red and brimstone. And the heads of the horses were like the heads of lions. And out of their mouths issued fire and smoke and brimstone.
By these three the third part of men was killed, by the fire, and by the smoke, and by the brimstone which issued out of their mouths.

For their authority is in their mouth and in
their tails. For their tails were like serpents
with heads, and with them they do harm."
(Revelation 9:13-19, MKJV)

A sudden global conflict, in which multiple nations
deploy their full military arsenals, could result in the deaths
of one-third of the world's population within a brief period.
According to the doctrine of Mutual Assured Destruction
(M.A.D.), hypersonic missiles can reach targets within one
hour, making a catastrophic loss of life possible in a very
short timeframe.

In the aftermath of such devastation, it is uncertain
whether humanity would turn to religious texts and seek
spiritual guidance. It remains to be seen if advocacy
groups, lobbyists, and other influential actors will
reconsider their positions and engage with scriptural
teachings. Furthermore, the question arises as to whether
governments would acknowledge the authority of religious
doctrine and its historical significance.

"And the rest of the men who were not killed
by these plagues still did not repent of the
works of their hands, that they should not
worship demons, and golden, and silver, and
bronze, and stone, and wooden idols (which
neither can see, nor hear, nor walk).
And they did not repent of their murders, nor
of their sorceries, nor of their fornication, nor
of their thefts."
(Revelation 9:20-21, MKJV)

Many individuals, especially soldiers and generals, place
great trust in military power. It is important to consider

whether they will reflect on the true causes of conflict, acknowledge their support for leadership seeking to acquire resources for personal gain, and reconsider any harmful motivations or animosity.

According to the Bible, they will not reflect on their actions or seek to develop a Godly character and the peace promoted by true Christianity. Instead, the preference for misguided interpretations of Christianity and other faiths that justify conflict and animosity will persist.

Apocalypse

Chapter 10

Prophesy Again

Tenth Commandment:
"You shall not covet your neighbor's house. You shall not covet your neighbor's wife, nor his manservant, nor his maidservant, nor his ox, nor his ass, nor anything that is your neighbor's."
(Exodus 20:17, MKJV)

(Coveting the riches of neighboring nation's resources often leads to wars. It has happened time and again in the past and will happen again.)

The first nine chapters of Revelation outline events from the era of the original apostles to a final world war, in which hypersonic missiles will trigger Mutual Assured Destruction. Within one hour, a third of humanity will perish, including both soldiers and civilians. The resulting devastation will cause widespread hunger and, in some regions, civil war.

How did this happen? Why do wars occur? Chapter ten pauses the sequence of events, but the remainder of Revelation provides further insight into the causes, explaining how humanity reaches the point of mutual destruction.

Revelation 10:1-11

"And I saw another mighty angel coming down
out of the heaven, clothed with a cloud. And a
rainbow was on his head, and his face was as
the sun, and his feet like pillars of fire.
And he had a little book open in his hand.
And he set his right foot on the sea and his
left foot on the earth.
And he cried with a loud voice, like a lion
roaring. And when he had cried, seven
thunders spoke their sounds.
And when the seven thunders spoke their
sounds, I was about to write. And I heard a
voice from Heaven saying to me, Seal up what
things the seven thunders spoke, and do not
write these things."
(Revelation 10:1-4, MKJV)

The indications here suggest a pause in the sequence. So
far, the book of Revelation has provided a framework for
what follows. This framework, like a skeleton, will now be
expanded with additional detail.

"And the angel whom I saw standing on the
sea and on the earth lifted his hand to the
heaven,
and swore by Him who lives forever and ever,
who created the heaven and the things in it,
and the earth and the things in it, and the sea
and the things in it, that there should no
longer be time.

But in the days of the voice of the seventh angel, when he will begin to sound, the mystery of God should be finished, as He has declared to His servants the prophets." (Revelation 10:5-7, MKJV)

Another declaration confirms the time sequence is complete, though specific details will follow. From the moment hypersonic missiles are launched, the return of the Messiah will be imminent. Revelation will provide further details and ultimately describe the Second Advent and its unfolding.

"And the voice which I heard from Heaven spoke to me again, and said, Go, take the little book which is open in the hand of the angel who stands on the sea and on the earth. And I went to the angel and said to him, Give me the little book. And he said to me, Take it and eat it up, and it will make your belly bitter, but it will be sweet as honey in your mouth.
And I took the little book out of the angel's hand and ate it up. And it was sweet as honey in my mouth, and as soon as I had eaten it, my belly was made bitter." (Revelation 10:8-10, MKJV)

The message in the remainder of Revelation was encouraging to the apostle John. It reveals that although humanity will falter, Jesus Christ will return at the appointed time to save humanity from destruction. John found hope in knowing his Messiah would return and restore all things, fulfilling his deepest hopes and efforts.

However, humanity remains resistant to salvation, choosing independence, as Adam and Eve did. Their desire for autonomy has, after nearly 6,000 years, led to the threat of global destruction. Despite the promise of the Messiah's return, significant hardship and bitterness still await those who reject guidance.

Ultimately, John was instructed to continue explaining how and why these events would unfold. He is now prepared to provide the necessary details to complete the initial outline.

> "And he said to me, You must prophesy again before many peoples and nations and tongues and kings."
> (Revelation 10:11, MKJV)

Chapter 11

Two Witnesses

The ministry of the Two Witnesses is now evident. In the Last Days, two witnesses will deliver a powerful message to the world using various media platforms. Modern technology, including satellites, television networks, and the Internet, enables this message to reach a global audience. While the prophet may not have foreseen these advancements, they now enable rapid news dissemination.

Initially, God will test true worshippers to determine their commitment to worship, adherence to His Commandments, and dedication to following His Son, Jesus Christ, in righteous living.

Revelation 11:1-2

"And a reed like a rod was given to me. And the angel stood, saying, Rise up and measure the temple of God, and the altar, and those who worship in it."
(Revelation 11:1, MKJV)

True worshippers may face challenges, but they are called to remain steadfast. Members of the Churches of God are tested to demonstrate the sincerity of their worship. Their loyalty and commitment to God's Commandments are essential for participation in the first resurrection and to rule with Christ during the seventh millennium following His return. This is discussed later in this book.

> "But leave out the court which is outside the temple, and do not measure it, for it was given to the nations. And they will trample the holy city forty-two months."
> (Revelation 11:2, MKJV)

This passage requires further clarification.

During the Old Testament era, the Temple in Jerusalem had a side court where uncircumcised gentiles could listen to sermons and observe rituals. However, they were not permitted to participate in rituals or receive full benefits, such as inheritance in the Promised Land. Circumcision was required for foreigners to access these privileges.

In the New Testament Christian era, many learn about the Gospel of the coming Kingdom of God. Those who become fully converted and circumcised in their hearts can repent of breaking God's Commandments. They may then be baptized and be assured of their future inheritance of eternal life.

However, few become fully converted, baptized, and remain committed to the Covenant. Most do not keep the fourth Commandment and misunderstand its importance, believing the Commandments are no longer required. As a result, they are not saved and will not be tested for their loyalty to the King and High Priest in this life.

This period refers to the three-and-a-half years of the Great Tribulation in the Last Days. During this time, many will hear the Gospel message through international evangelistic efforts but may not respond positively to the opportunity God offers. Only a few will repent and become fully converted. Unless they become circumcised in their heart to take the steps to fully enter the spiritual Temple of the Churches of God, they may easily leave, and even trample on the Gospel. That is, unfortunately, the case for most in the world. They hear the Gospel, understand enough, but fail to commit. They trample on the opportunity to inherit eternal life.

In a broader sense, the world will frantically search for salvation during WW3 and will search for Godly protection, but will they repent and live a sacrificial life? Hence, the outer court will symbolically be overrun by the world, with many trampling the opportunity, unwilling to do what is required for salvation. They are not under scrutiny by the Angels for loyalty to Christ in keeping the Commandments, but are afforded the opportunity to understand the true Gospel message of the literal coming of the Kingdom of God, when Christ returns. These will be in a later resurrection at the end of the millennial rule of Christ on the earth, as we will see later in this book.

Revelation 11:3-14

The preaching of the Gospel to the world at large in the Great Tribulation is strengthened by the arrival of the Two Witnesses.

"And I will give power to My two witnesses, and they will prophesy a thousand, two hundred and sixty days, clothed in sackcloth." (Revelation 11:3, MKJV)

Who are the Two Witnesses? The Bible explains.

Jesus presented several apostles with a vision of a future event known as "The Transfiguration." In this vision, Jesus appeared resurrected and glorified. The apostles saw Him with the Two Witnesses and witnessed a preview of the Kingdom of Heaven on earth. Please consider the following vision:

> "And He said to them, Truly I say to you that there are some of those who stand here who shall not taste of death until they see the kingdom of God come with power.
> And after six days Jesus took Peter and James and John and led them up into a high mountain, apart by themselves. And He was transfigured before them.
> And His clothing became shining, exceedingly white as snow such as no fuller on earth could whiten them.
> And Elijah with Moses was seen by them, and they were talking with Jesus."
> (Mark 9:1-4, MKJV)

They saw Elijah and Moses resurrected as the Two Witnesses. Through their prior ministries and sufferings, they demonstrated an unwavering commitment to worship and obedience to God.

Moses served as a civil leader, while Elijah was a prophet. Historically, state and religion were separate, but in Jesus Christ, these roles are unified. In the future Kingdom of God, this unity will extend to the resurrected saints. Initially, however, the resurrected Two Witnesses will address global corruption in state and religion separately during the Great Tribulation.

The remainder of the chapter explains how nations and peoples will be compelled to confront the corruption in religious and civil leadership. These resurrected leaders will resemble Christ after His resurrection: able to walk the earth and eat, yet possessing power far beyond human capability.

"These are the two olive trees and the two lampstands standing before the God of the earth.
And if anyone will hurt them, fire proceeds out of their mouth and devours their enemies. And if anyone will hurt them, so it is right for him to be killed.
These have authority to shut up the heaven, that it may not rain in the days of their prophecy. And they have authority over waters to turn them to blood, and to strike the earth with every plague, as often as they desire."
(Revelation 11:4-6, MKJV)

They will be empowered to compel nations to heed the Word of God. A significant effort will be made to encourage more people to listen to Him. God desires to offer eternal life to all, but this requires worship, obedience, and adherence to His Commandments. Individuals must also respect and follow His Son, Jesus Christ, and refrain from blaspheming His Name. The Witnesses will conduct their ministry from Jerusalem.

However, the war machines of the world will come to Jerusalem, and God will allow the Two Witnesses to become martyrs, so that the world can understand just how bad the corrupt leaders of the world are. The false religious leaders will expose themselves. The soldiers will be ashamed of their crimes against humanity. They still think their war machine can destroy any foreign invader. So God will allow the Two Witnesses to die before the war machine, just as He allowed the One from Heaven, Jesus the Christ, to die. But it will be temporary.

> "And when they complete their testimony, the beast coming up out of the abyss will make war against them and will overcome them and kill them.
> And their bodies will lie in the street of the great city, which spiritually is called Sodom and Egypt, where also our Lord was crucified. And many of the peoples and tribes and tongues and nations will see their dead bodies three days and a half, and they will not allow their dead bodies to be put in tombs.
> And the ones who dwell on the earth will rejoice over them, and will make merry, and will send one another gifts, because these two prophets tormented those living on the earth."
> (Revelation 11:7-10, MKJV)

People will demonstrate how bad they are. The disobedient godless people who hate all religions will rejoice, but only for a few days. The world has not studied and proven the one true religion. They are not able to distinguish. Due to a lack of knowledge, they have even banned the Bible from schools. They have even banned a display of the Ten Commandments. But in their rebellion, they allow sin and crime, leading to civil strife, even civil war, and ultimately world wars. It has to stop.

The Two Witnesses are the resurrected Moses and Elijah, and are fully capable of rising again in total astonishment for fleshly people.

> "And after three days and a half, a spirit of
> life from God entered into them, and they
> stood on their feet. And great fear fell on those
> seeing them.
> And they heard a great voice from Heaven
> saying to them, Come up here. And they went
> up to Heaven in a cloud, and their enemies
> watched them.
> And in that hour a great earthquake occurred,
> and the tenth part of the city fell. And seven
> thousand names of men were slain in the
> earthquake. And the rest were frightened and
> gave glory to the God of Heaven.
> The second woe passed away. Behold, the
> third woe comes quickly."
> (Revelation 11:11-14, MKJV)

Many will repent and begin to really worship God. Some will become obedient, reach out to God's mercy, and keep His Commandments and follow Jesus Christ. They will no longer deny Him. This is how God will begin to prepare for the coming Kingdom of God, when Jesus Christ will rule from Jerusalem. These things will happen, just as it is written in your Bible.

Ultimately, God will reign through Jesus Christ from Jerusalem. Pollution by industry chiefs and the rich will stop. Corrupt civil leaders and false religious teachers will stop. Utopia will come, and paradise can flourish again.

The Two Witnesses would have managed to turn the world around towards worshipping the Creator God and following the risen Christ. Jesus with Moses and Elijah will have conquered the world, and the seventh millennium will have started.

Revelation 11:15-19

The seventh angel is now able to sound the seventh trumpet, signifying the ultimate proclamation of the arrival of Jesus Christ. The heavenly host expresses great jubilation.

"And the seventh angel sounded. And there were great voices in Heaven, saying, The kingdoms of this world have become the kingdoms of our Lord, and of His Christ. And He will reign forever and ever.
And the twenty-four elders sitting before God on their thrones, fell on their faces and worshiped God,
Saying, We thank You, O Lord God Almighty, who are, and who was, and who is coming, because You took Your great power and reigned.
And the nations were full of wrath, and Your wrath came, and the time of the judging of the dead, and to give the reward to Your servants the prophets, and to the saints, and to the ones fearing Your name, to the small and to the great, and to destroy those destroying the earth.

And the temple of God was opened in Heaven, and there was seen in His temple the ark of His covenant, and there occurred lightnings and voices, and thunders and an earthquake, and a great hail."
(Revelation 11:15-19, MKJV)

Summary

God intervened in the powers, allowing the Two Witnesses to directly address the world and its leaders, exposing their failures. Wars will only stop once the world understands their war machines are useless against God and His resurrected leaders. The people of the world will ultimately ignore their corrupt leaders and become unified in the worship of God and His Commandments.

The world needs to see and understand that God's Commandments are eternal. The world must be in awe of God and His Covenant with humanity. Humans must fear the breaking of the Covenant. We must all worship God, keep His Commandments, and follow His Son, Jesus the Christ, the only Messiah.

Apocalypse

Chapter 12

Christ's Victory

Chapter 12 revealed the path of Christ and the Church of God to ultimate salvation. It provides background spiritual information on the Messiah's first advent, subsequent atrocities against the saints and wars, and the run-up to His Second Advent. More detail is provided concerning what happened in Heaven at the time of the Messiah's First and Second Advents. For God and His Throne, these are momentous events.

Symbols of the sun, moon, woman, and stars are used. We need to let the Bible again interpret these for us. Consider another passage that uses these symbols. Understand the symbolism:

"And he dreamed still another dream, and told it to his brothers. And he said, Behold, I have dreamed another dream. And behold, the sun and the moon and the eleven stars bowed down to me.
And he told it to his father and to his brothers. And his father rebuked him and said to him, What is this dream that you have dreamed? Shall I, and your mother, and your brothers indeed come to bow ourselves to the earth before you?"
(Genesis 37:9-10, MKJV)

The sun refers to the father, in this case, the patriarch. The moon refers to the mother and woman, the one who gave life to the family, the home-maker. She reflects sunlight. The stars refer to children who came from the woman. In this case, in Genesis, it clearly refers to the twelve brothers, of which Joseph was one, leaving the other eleven that would bow to their brother when they came to seek food during a time of severe drought.

Now consider the vision given to the apostle John as shown in Chapter 12.

Revelation 12:1

"And there appeared a great sign in the
heavens, a woman clothed with the sun, and
the moon was under her feet, and a crown of
twelve stars on her head,
(Revelation 12:1, MKJV)

First, consider that the sun symbolizes the Heavenly Father. His righteousness shines forth and lights the path for angels and people to walk in peace. His ways, Commandments, and Laws are a light for all. There are many verses that make this clear. Just consider the following piece of Godly wisdom:

"My son, keep your father's commandments,
and do not forsake the law of your mother;
bind them upon your heart forever, tie them
around your neck.
When you go, it shall lead you; when you
sleep, it shall keep you; and when you awake,
it shall talk with you.
For the commandment is a lamp; and the law
is light; and reproofs of instruction are the
way of life;"

(Proverbs 6:20-23, MKJV)

The moon, as a light-reflecting object, symbolizes the center of the religion. In the Old Testament, it represents the Levitical priesthood and the Temple services in Jerusalem led by the high priest. The woman symbolizes the rabbis and preachers in Jerusalem, from whom would emerge spiritual offspring. Although the woman and the moon are conceptually intertwined, each carries a distinct emphasis while contributing to a common purpose. The moon is not an appropriate symbol for a pregnant woman capable of bearing a son; therefore, the woman and the moon are depicted together, forming a suitable symbol for the anticipated miracle.

The twelve stars in the Old Testament represent the twelve tribes of Israel and their leaders. In the New Testament, they signify the twelve apostles and their followers.

The sun illuminates the woman, the moon, and the stars—interpreted as apostles and disciples—who reflect righteousness as well as the Commandments and Laws of God. The prophecy of Daniel concerning the Last Days is particularly relevant in this context:

"And those who are wise shall shine as the brightness of the sky; and those who turn many to righteousness shall shine as the stars forever and ever."
(Daniel 12:3, MKJV)

The woman with her feet on the moon will now produce the most important offspring ever! Into this structure, another great wonder happened. Someone perfect in all His ways would need to live as a human, yet obey God perfectly. He would have to be the personification of

God. After His death He would not be left to waste away in a grave. He would be raised to live forever as our High Priest in Heaven. Such a completely perfect being was required to lead sinning humans to the sinless life in God's Kingdom.

Such a sinless individual would show His love in His ultimate sacrifice. He would be in the Temple in Jerusalem, yet rejected and persecuted by a corrupt priesthood consisting of mere humans. He would be killed by a corrupt occupying leadership, representing a world empire. Such an event did happen. Such a sacrificial life did walk the streets of Jerusalem. Jesus was born into that situation near Jerusalem. He was born of Mary, but He was born out of the need of a saviour for Jews and Gentiles. The prophets declared His arrival. Those in Jerusalem expected His arrival. Even the priests were well aware of the timing. Even wise men from the east came to Bethlehem to find Him. One could say Jerusalem was "pregnant" with expectancy.

Revelation 12:2-6

"and having a babe in womb, she cries, being in travail, having been distressed to bear."
(Revelation 12:2, MKJV)

Will the Levitical Priesthood accept Him with open arms? Will the Roman Empire accept him with open arms? The devil made sure they didn't.

"And another sign was seen in the heavens. And behold a great red dragon, having seven heads and ten horns and seven crowns on his heads!"
(Revelation 12:3, MKJV)

The heads, horns, and crowns refer to successive world empires mentioned elsewhere, all instituted by the devil who opposes God. Some are mentioned in Daniel as they ruled up until the First Advent of the Messiah. This is described in the book on Daniel's Timeline.

More world empires would follow after the First Advent, and some are described in Revelation in subsequent chapters.

A brief description of a previous event is provided to identify who the dragon is and his effect on the world. Satan deceived Adam and Eve, but previously deceived some angels to follow him instead of God.

This Satan is influencing, and in devious ways, ruling over some kings of countries and world empires. He is described as the King of Tyre in Ezekiel 28:11-19. He corrupted himself and also misled a third of the angels, who became demons. They were cast out to the earth, banished from God's Throne.

"And his tail drew the third part of the stars of heaven, and cast them onto the earth. And the dragon stood before the woman being about to bear, so that when she bears he might devour her child."
(Revelation 12:4, MKJV)

Satan moved Herod to kill Jesus after His birth, but the parents of Jesus were led to flee Judea and hide in Egypt till Herod lost his mind and died, after which his son took over. This is described in Matthew chapter two. Therefore, Jesus survived. He began His ministry at 30, as required by the Law. His ministry was cut short after three and a half years; He was crucified as prophesied in Daniel, resurrected three nights and three days later as per the prophet Jonah, and taken to Heaven.

> "And she bore a son, a male, who is going to rule all nations with a rod of iron. And her child was caught up to God and to His throne."
> (Revelation 12:5, MKJV)

The four Gospels describe this in detail. Ruling with a rod of iron signifies unwavering obedience to God's Law. Many governments use a hollow golden rod in ceremonies to symbolize the constitution that leaders pledge to uphold. Jesus the Messiah would uphold God's constitution as outlined in the Bible. He will rule with that rod of iron.

Next, the Church that now replaced the Temple service was warned about the coming destruction of Jerusalem. They fled to the mountains at the right time, probably to the rock city among the hills, named Petra.

> "And the woman fled into the wilderness, where she had a place prepared by God, so that they might nourish her there a thousand, two hundred and sixty days."
> (Revelation 12:6, MKJV)

It is possible that most of the Church initially stayed in Petra for 1260 days before it was safe to return to Jerusalem. The reference here is exact. The Church had to flee, and Petra was available to migrants as an independent city. It was in the wilderness, and its unique features provided safety from Roman soldiers. It has one entrance through a split in some huge boulders, and the defenders could pick off soldiers one by one as they came in. It was a death trap for an army. It was as if the city of Petra was prepared by God to provide a safe place for the Church.

After the sacrifice of Jesus Christ, the apostles could preach in power and call disciples to repentance. Humans now have the power to resist the devil and demons. Satan no longer had a place in heaven.

Revelation 12:7-14

"And there was war in Heaven. Michael and his angels warring against the dragon. And the dragon and his angels warred,
but did not prevail. Nor was place found for them in Heaven any more.
And the great dragon was cast out, the old serpent called Devil, and Satan, who deceives the whole world. He was cast out into the earth, and his angels were cast out with him.
And I heard a great voice saying in Heaven, Now has come the salvation and power and the kingdom of our God, and the authority of His Christ. For the accuser of our brothers is cast down, who accused them before our God day and night.
And they overcame him because of the blood of the Lamb, and because of the word of their testimony. And they did not love their soul until death.
Therefore rejoice, O heavens, and those tabernacling in them. Woe to the inhabitants of the earth and in the sea! For the Devil came down to you, having great wrath, knowing that he has but a little time."

(Revelation 12:7-12, MKJV)

Satan went out to cause war time and again. Often, cities were destroyed, rebuilt by successive generations, and destroyed again.

"And when the dragon saw that he was cast to the earth, he persecuted the woman who bore the man child. And two wings of a great eagle were given to the woman, so that she might fly into the wilderness, into her place, where she is nourished for a time and times and half a time, from the serpent's face."
(Revelation 12:13-14, MKJV)

The Church of God had to flee many times. From the mid-4th century till the 1600s, the Church was oppressed. A time refers to a year. Times refer to two years. Half a time obviously refers to half a year, or six months. The day-for-a-year principle applies, as shown in Ezekiel 4:6. A year in prophecy equals 360 days. Thus, we need to add the days. We need to add 3.5 years in days, which equals 1260 days. Then apply the prophetic-day-for-a-year principle, and we have 1260 years.

This formed the 1260 years of the Dark Middle Ages of Europe, till God allowed the pandemic to wipe out millions of people. At that time, the false churches lost their hold on Europe, and the Reformation could happen. People were allowed to receive the Bible in their home languages. The light of God's Word and Commandments could shine again, pushing out the Dark Middle Ages.

For 1260 years, the Church often had to flee the cities where it was established. Then they had to survive in the countryside. This has been the usual case in Europe. Many times God heard the prayers of the saints and allowed wars in Europe to punish those regimes that persecuted the Church. Finally, the church could flee to the "free worlds" and establish religious freedom in English-speaking nations through the constitutions that city leaders had to adhere to.

A period of religious freedom was established. This was in accordance with events that played out in Heaven. From the Middle East, wars would ensue that reached the "free worlds" of the English-speaking nations. However, the earth helped the "free worlds" and therefore the Churches of God that grew in those countries. Often, weather played a big role in battles, ensuring that the "free worlds" retained religious freedom till the end. It was the time of European colonisation of Africa, the Americas, and even Australia and New Zealand. There was a history of Sabbath churches that fled persecution in Europe, which was erased from history lessons in various schools and libraries. Wars ensued regularly in colonies across the world. Some European nations, like France recently admitted their atrocities, but will the churches of Europe own up to their persecutions? Some things are better left unsaid to try to protect the unity of European church organisations. However, the Bible correctly prophesied about these oppressions worldwide.

From Europe, soldiers motivated by false church leaders who moved civil rulers towards war were sent to the "free worlds" where the true Church could worship, keeping the Commandments of God. Identification is clear, particularly through the fourth Commandment. The massive number of soldiers went forth like rivers to travel to strange countries where they met inclement weather and diseases, and they failed to conquer the English-speaking "free worlds" to subdue and banish freedom of religion. So these soldiers mainly succeeded in preventing the true Worship from spreading back home in Europe.

Revelation 12:15-17

"And the serpent cast out of his mouth water like a flood after the woman, so that he might cause her to be carried away by the river. And the earth helped the woman. And the earth opened its mouth and swallowed up the river which the dragon cast out of his mouth. And the dragon was enraged over the woman, and went to make war with the rest of her seed, who keep the commandments of God and have the testimony of Jesus Christ." (Revelation 12:15-17, MKJV)

The Church keeps the Ten Commandments of God. This verse clearly identifies the true worshippers from the false congregations. Churches that preach that the Ten Commandments are done away with are clearly exposed as false. Their doctrines and actions are to be questioned in the face of evidence and even history. A clear understanding of the Bible is undeniable. The prophecies proved true and were fulfilled.

Chapter 13

Gentile Kingdoms

Revelation 13:1

Chapter 13 provides details about the Gentile kingdoms that would affect Jerusalem, and in particular the Church of God, from the time of the apostle John and the crucifixion until the Second Advent and the beginning of the rule of Christ from Jerusalem.

> "And I stood on the sand of the sea, and I saw a beast coming up out of the sea, having seven heads and ten horns. And on its horns were ten crowns, and on its heads was the name of blasphemy."
> (Revelation 13:1, MKJV)

Water often represents a mass of people. A beast out of the sea represents a ruthless government forming. It also indicates a seafaring army being sent across the Mediterranean Sea to invade Israel from the east. This was the classical invasion from Rome.

The seven heads are seen as successive incarnations of the world-ruling empire, and, in this case, are generally understood as the Roman Empire.

Horns are offensive weapons. They denote military powers. Ten horns are the ten generals of ten countries or provinces in Europe. Their borders are not the borders of today, but rather as they were initially, which may be reinstated in the Last Days due to wars over borders. Numerous wars in Europe have redrawn borders many times since the beginning. Therefore, don't expect to be able to label ten current countries of Europe. Watch the wars in the Middle East and the results of alliances.

The ten crowns are the ten kings, rulers, or senates that form the group that, together, constitute the total EU government in the Middle Europe. Blasphemy refers directly to cursing God or Christ. It also refers to the Hollywood language of some idols. It can also refer to the subtlety of being called "Christian" but not acting accordingly, thereby blaspheming the Name of Christ. Such people do not keep the Commandments of God, particularly the fourth Commandment, which identifies true worshippers. This beast would then form their own religions and develop a hybrid of their former pagan gods and true Christianity, thereby calling themselves Christian, but they are not. They even promote gay rights and gay pride events and symbols, and will allow other forms of religions to have equal power as Christianity, even standing by while true Christianity is oppressed. So they are indeed blasphemous. Notice how Jesus was accused of blasphemy because He claimed to be from God. But history has proved Jesus to be true, and those who accused Him are shown to be false, and hence blasphemers.

> "do you say of Him whom the Father has sanctified and sent into the world, You blaspheme, because I said, I am the Son of God?"
> (John 10:36, MKJV)

An empire that claims to be Christian, but breaks the Commandments and even persecutes those who try to reform its religious institution is indeed blasphemous.

Revelation 13:2-5

"And the beast which I saw was like a leopard, and its feet like those of a bear, and its mouth like the mouth of a lion. And the dragon gave him its power and its seat and great authority."
(Revelation 13:2, MKJV).

The nature of this world empire, which periodically influenced Jerusalem and oppressed the Church of God, is depicted as a beast that consumes other nations, governments, and religious organizations. Despite its efforts, it was unable to eradicate Christianity. The empire is described as being driven by Satan, symbolized as the dragon, and consequently persecuted Christian Sabbatarian worshippers.

The attributes of the three preceding empires are combined in the fourth beast. The first attribute, resembling a leopard, signifies cunning and the ability to outmaneuver adversaries. The second attribute, akin to a bear, represents power and persistence, as it tenaciously holds its prey. The lion-like mouth symbolizes the projection of authority and dominance over its territories and subjects.

"And I saw one of its heads as having been slain to death, and its deadly wound was

healed. And all the earth marveled after the beast."
(Revelation 13:3, MKJV)

There has been speculation regarding the identity of the king referenced in this verse, with Emperor Nero considered a leading candidate. Nero ruled during the early spread of Christianity throughout the Roman Empire. Influenced by sun worshippers, he initiated a persecution against Christians, allowing Rome to burn and then blaming Christians for the disaster, leading to their martyrdom. Nero ultimately suffered mental decline and was restrained by his deputies until his death. It is rumored that he committed suicide by falling on his sword, possibly with assistance from a deputy.

Many expected Rome to fall and the Empire to disintegrate, but political leaders maintained its stability. They adopted elements of the Christian faith, suggesting that Nero was in heaven and still ruling. As a result, homage was paid to the next Emperor as if Nero still directed the Empire. These were traumatic times for Christians, who viewed these events as the fulfillment of prophecy.

Rather than embracing Christianity, Romans intensified their sun worship, observing practices such as Sunday and Saturnalia, the mid-December festival welcoming the sun's return to the northern hemisphere. Many continued to revere Nero in spirit, as if he were still alive.

"And they worshiped the dragon who gave authority to the beast. And they worshiped

the beast, saying, Who is like the beast? Who is able to make war with it?"
(Revelation 13:4, MKJV)

The dragon refers to Satan and his false religion. Satan wants to be revered as Christ. Through cunning references, he made pagan religions and practices appear Christian by naming pagan festivals as if they were Christian ones. Therefore, the leaders of the sun worshiping religion moved the Roman authorities to even directly oppose true Christians and persecute them. They would even ridicule true Christian leaders.

"And a mouth speaking great things was given to it, and blasphemies. And authority was given to it to continue forty-two months."
(Revelation 13:5, MKJV)

The forty-two months needs to be seen as 42x30 days, which is 1260 days. Then the day for a year principle in prophecy needs to be applied, arriving at a period of 1260 years of the Dark Middle Ages of Europe, where nobody were allowed to have a Bible to read it for themselves.

Revelation 13:6-8

"And it opened its mouth in blasphemy toward God, to blaspheme His name and His tabernacle, and those dwelling in Heaven. And it was given to it to war with the saints and to overcome them. And authority was

given to it over every tribe and tongue and nation."
(Revelation 13:6-7, MKJV)

This showed the extent of European colonisation and rule. Compromised Christianity was exported to the world, and is evident worldwide. Those that blindly follow the compromised religion will unfortunately not have their name written in the Book of Life. They will have to redo their search for the true Worship again in the second resurrection.

"And all dwelling on the earth will worship it, those whose names have not been written in the Book of Life of the Lamb slain, from the foundation of the world."
(Revelation 13:8, MKJV)

To understand about the Resurrections, see the book on Life after Death.

https://www.amazon.com/gp/product/B08CL3ZG1B?ref_= dbs_m_mng_rwt_calw_tkin_11&storeType=ebooks

Revelation 13:9-11

The saints are cautioned to be patient while in their oppression. They must not seek revenge, nor give up and compromise with their Faith. They are promised that God will exact a penalty from the oppressors. They will suffer in the same way that they are persecuting the Christians.

"If anyone has an ear, let him hear.

He who leads into captivity will go into
captivity. If anyone will kill with the sword, he
must be killed by a sword. Here is the
patience and the faith of the saints."
(Revelation 13:9-10, MKJV)

So true Christians suffering persecution can rest
assure that those who cause them harm will ultimately
suffer the same. As Rome caused Christians to suffer in
those days, war came to Rome and they suffered the same.

"And I saw another beast coming up out of the
earth. And it had two horns like a lamb, and
he spoke like a dragon."
(Revelation 13:11, MKJV)

This beast may appear like a lamb. It seems harmless at
first. It may be seen as following the Lamb, Jesus Christ. It
may even try to pretend to be the resurrected Lamb. In its
ultimate form, it will claim the authority of the Lamb in
order to change religious laws, even changing from
Sabbath to Sunday. But it is deceived and carries on with
the same wrong doctrines of the sun-worship religion. This
was particularly the case after the 4th-century political coup
that established Christianity as the official religion.

Sometimes this is also evident in false churches that at
first act blasphemously by claiming to be Christian yet
denying the full and true worship. Once they are proven
false, then instead of repenting, they could openly
blaspheme the name of God and His Son. How is the name
of Jesus Christ not blasphemed today by Hollywood idols
who themselves promote fornication and gay marriages?
The blasphemy has no end! Such was the case also in the
Roman Empire.

Revelation 13:12-18

The blasphemy in Rome, therefore, reached a sophistication in the 4th century, when the Roman authorities, under the guidance of Emperor Constantine, developed a compromise that mixed Christianity with paganism and sun god worship. A new mixed religion was enforced in the Roman Empire, vexing the saints and overcoming them. At first, Christians were invited to the new mixed religion, then forced to worship with the pagans, and then persecuted if they refused to compromise with the pure Christian Faith.

> "And it exercises all the authority of the first beast before him, and causes the earth and those dwelling in it to worship the first beast, whose deadly wound was healed.
> And it does great wonders, so that it makes fire come down from the heaven onto the earth in the sight of men.
> And it deceives those dwelling on the earth, because of the miracles which were given to it to do before the beast, saying to those dwelling on the earth that they should make an image to the beast who had the wound by a sword and lived."
> (Revelation 13:12-14, MKJV)

At times, the Pope of Rome competed with the Emperor for authority. Even so, successive Emperors beseech the Pope to crown them. In such cases, the Papal authorities even gain power over the Emperor to obey their desire to eradicate true Christianity. So, in the same way as the beast before actually continues, oppressing those who don't follow the mindset and ways of their leadership. They will find that the leadership is a beast that will oppress and destroy.

> "And there was given to it to give a spirit to
> the image of the beast, so that the image of
> the beast might both speak, and might cause
> as many as would not worship the image of
> the beast to be killed."
> (Revelation 13:15, MKJV)

The "Christian" Europe was moved by the church to worship the Emperor as the one sanctioned by God, and the church and state became one oppressive beast. It happened in the Dark Middle Ages. It may happen again as Europe tries to contain Islamification. And how will they kill their opponents? Starvation? Loss of jobs? Jailed in horrible conditions? Refusal of access to needed medication? Through economic sanctions, even at the individual level.

> "And it causes all, both small and great, rich
> and poor, free and bond, to receive a mark on
> their right hand, or in their foreheads,
> even that not any might buy or sell except
> those having the mark, or the name of the
> beast, or the number of its name."
> (Revelation 13:16-17, MKJV)

Finally the beast that ruins those who don't worship it is cleverly identified.

> "Here is the wisdom. Let him having reason
> count the number of the beast, for it is the

number of a man. And its number is six
hundred and sixty-six."
(Revelation 13:18, MKJV)

Various names have been shown to fulfill this verse if the letters of their names are replaced with the corresponding Roman numerals and added up. There could also be elements of the idea that identify it with a leader who promotes keeping the sixth day of the week, but that is speculation. In some Greek manuscripts, the number was changed to 616. So, in Hebrew, it is 666, and in some Greek, it is 616. In Hebrew, the name is Neron Qesar, and in Greek it is Nero Caesar. If that is taken into account, the only name that matches it all is Nero Caesar. However, all other attempts still seem to point to a Roman Empire leader. Nero started, and others followed the same path through the centuries. What is certain is the identification of the Bible as such.

God gave humankind six days in which to work and fulfill their own purposes. But the seventh day belongs to God. In that God expects us to listen to Him in order to fashion our lives according to His Commandments and Law.

Six is often the number of humankind trying to make it on their own without God. Seven is often the number of perfection in God. It shows that we are not perfect by our own devices. We need God to show us the perfect and permanent way that leads to eternal life. Six is the number of a manmade government and a manmade religion. Seven is the number of a Godly religion, and will be the number of Jesus Christ's reign from Jerusalem.

Chapter 14

Harvesting Saints

Chapter 14 describes two stages in the gathering of saints for eternal service with Jesus Christ during His millennial reign. True worshippers are sealed through steadfast love, worship, and obedience to God and His Commandments, even in the face of temptation and opposition. They consistently stand for God.

During the Old Testament era, the invitation to worship and inherit eternal life was extended to the Israelites and the Gentiles among them. Following Israel's dispersion by Nebuchadnezzar, the prophesied restoration occurred in Daniel's time. Those restored to Judea were primarily from the tribes of Judah, Levi, and some from Benjamin, collectively known as Jews at the Messiah's First Advent. Many, including some Gentiles, repented and were given the opportunity to worship fully through Jesus Christ.

In the New Testament era, worship for all is through Jesus Christ, the crucified and resurrected Messiah and our High Priest. This applies to both Jews and Gentiles. While Jews may retain their physical inheritance in the Promised Land through circumcision, repentance and forgiveness for both groups come only through Christ, whose death atones for our former sins.

Revelation 14:1

Repentant Jews and Gentiles who remain faithful and keep the Commandments until death are sealed and will be gathered at the first resurrection when the Messiah returns.

"And I looked, and lo, the Lamb stood on Mount Zion. And with Him were a hundred and forty-four thousands, having His Father's name written in their foreheads."
(Revelation 14:1, MKJV)

This is the first category. As another verse shows, these are Jews who fully accept Jesus as Christ and repented at the feet of the Crucified Messiah. They overcome their sin daily by considering the blood of the Messiah shed for their past sins.

"And I heard the number of those who were sealed, one hundred and forty-four thousands, having been sealed out of every tribe of the sons of Israel."
(Revelation 7:14, MKJV)

They fully accepted the New Covenant terms and are of the New Testament. Therefore, they know and can sing a new song. Resurrected true worshippers from the Old Testament era also see the Messiah and learn the new song, the New Testament.

Revelation14:2-3

"And I heard a voice from Heaven, like the voice of many waters and like the voice of a great thunder. And I heard the voice of harpers harping with their harps.
And they sang as it were a new song before the throne and before the four living creatures and the elders. And no one could learn that song except the hundred and forty-four thousands who were redeemed from the earth."
(Revelation 14:2-3, MKJV)

The promises to the patriarchs were firstly to Israel and beyond them also to the gentiles.

"But to those who indeed disobeying the truth out of self-seeking, and obeying unrighteousness, will be anger and wrath, tribulation and anguish upon every soul of man who has worked out evil; of the Jew first, and also of the Greek. But He will give glory, honor and peace to every man who works good, to the Jew first and also to the Greek."
(Romans 2:8-10, MKJV)

This chapter demonstrates that 144,000 Jews will be sealed by worshipping God and His Law, repenting before the Messiah. They accept forgiveness through the crucifixion and overcome sin through the blood of Jesus Christ, recognizing Him as their eternal High Priest.

It is essential to study the Word of God and worship Him directly through His Son, Jesus Christ. Individuals should not assume their chosen worship organization is correct. Throughout history, including in Judea during Jesus's time, there were many groups, such as the Pharisees, Sadducees, Zealots, and Essenes, and many made mistakes. God warns against blindly following any organization. While some organizations may offer immediate benefits, those who seek only these rewards will not inherit the eternal kingdom of God. God expects direct worship and a sincere love for His Commandments.

"However, they worship Me in vain, teaching
for doctrines the commandments of men."
For laying aside the commandment of God,
you hold the tradition of men, the dippings of
pots and cups. And many other such things
you do.
And He said to them, Do you do well to set
aside the commandment of God, so that you
may keep your own tradition?"
(Mark 7:7-9, MKJV)

Worshipping a religious organization that places manmade rules above God's Commandments and laws is cautioned against. Both Jews and Gentiles are encouraged to worship God through Jesus Christ and to prioritize the Word of God over organizational documents.

Revelation 14:4-7

"These are those who were not defiled with
women; for they are virgins. These are those
who follow the Lamb wherever He goes. These

were redeemed from among men, as a firstfruit to God and to the Lamb.
And in their mouth was found no guile, for they were without blemish before the throne of God."
(Revelation 14:4-5, MKJV)

And so the Jewish Christians are sealed and harvested first. But God's mercy extends to everybody.

"And I saw another angel flying in mid-heaven, having the everlasting gospel to preach to those dwelling on the earth, even to every nation and kindred and tongue and people,
saying with a great voice, Fear God and give glory to Him! For the hour of His judgment has come. And worship Him who made the heaven and the earth, and the sea, and the fountains of waters."
(Revelation 14:6-7, MKJV)

The message is intended for people worldwide. Christian evangelists are active globally, following God's direction and Jesus' leadership from Heaven.

However, many churches and organizations have adopted practices that are not authentic to the original faith. This issue dates back thousands of years, even before the time of Jesus Christ. For example, the king of Babylon observed the worship system in Jerusalem and created a similar but counterfeit system in Babylon, which later influenced major empires, including Rome. Over time, this hybrid system shaped the beliefs and practices of many societies. It is essential to address and overcome these influences so that individuals can worship God authentically, follow the true Messiah, and remain steadfast in the face of challenges, ultimately preparing for the Kingdom of God.

Revelation 14:8-16

"And another angel followed, saying, The great city, Babylon, has fallen, has fallen; because of the wine of the anger of her fornication; she has made all nations to drink."
(Revelation 14:8, MKJV)

Babylon and her false religious system had fallen long before the apostle John wrote this prophecy. However, it will be rebuilt in the Last Days and will fall again, hence the double curse pronounced here.

"And a third angel followed them, saying with a great voice, If anyone worships the beast and its image, and receives a mark in his forehead or in his hand,
he also will drink of the wine of the anger of God, having been mixed undiluted in the cup of His wrath. And he will be tormented by fire and brimstone before the holy angels, and in the presence of the Lamb.
And the smoke of their torment goes up forever and ever. And they have no rest day or night, those who worship the beast and its image, and whoever receives the mark of its name."
(Revelation 14:9-11, MKJV)

Apocalypse

Wars will come. Kingdoms formed on mankind's ideas and frankly corrupt ways will fail. People will suffer. Meanwhile the saints will worship God and keep His Commandments.

"Here is the patience of the saints. Here are
the ones who keep the commandments of God
and the faith of Jesus.
And I heard a voice from Heaven saying to me,
Write, Blessed are the dead who die in the
Lord from now on. Yes, says the Spirit, they
shall rest from their labors, and their works
follow them."
(Revelation 14:12-13, MKJV)

During the wars of the Last Days, Jesus will know who is truly following His Father in Heaven, and studied to undo deception in order to worship directly and according to His Will. He will harvest the true followers in the resurrection.

"And I looked, and behold, a white cloud. And
on the cloud sat one like the Son of man,
having a golden crown on His head, and a
sharp sickle in His hand.
And another angel came out of the temple,
crying in a great voice to Him sitting on the
cloud, Thrust in Your sickle and reap, for the
time has come for You to reap, for the harvest
of the earth was dried.
And He sitting on the cloud thrust in His
sickle on the earth, and the earth was
reaped."
(Revelation 14:14-16, MKJV)

As wars, problems and oppression spread worldwide to all nations, those who keep the Commandments and stay true to Jesus Christ is known to Messiah and He will harvest them for the first resurrection. This is explained in chapter 20.

Revelation 14:17-20

Finally there will be another harvesting of unrepentant people at the catastrophic world war at the end. A Great Tribulation will happen. Many will kill their fellow human beings in neighbourhood countries. They will kill and be killed.

"And another angel came out of the temple in Heaven, also having a sharp sickle.
And another angel came out from the altar, who had authority over fire. And he spoke with a great cry to him who had the sharp sickle, saying, Thrust in your sharp sickle, and gather the clusters of the vine of the earth, for her grapes are fully ripe.
And the angel thrust in his sickle into the earth and gathered the vine of the earth, and cast it into the great winepress of the anger of God.
And the winepress was trodden outside the city, and blood came out of the winepress, even to the bridles of the horses, for the space of a thousand, six hundred stadia."
(Revelation 14:17-20, MKJV)

Christ did not harvest these souls. Another angel did. They worshiped false gods. They worshiped fake religions. They worshiped false leaders that was antichrist and furthered their own agenda. They also worshiped idols of sport and music. Many worshiped themselves. Their worship led to animosity, intolerance, crime, and war. It did not lead to seeking God's wisdom, peace, and salvation.

Ultimate Messiah will return to stop the madness. The process of humankind's failure is shown in the next few chapters. The ultimate return of the Messiah and how he will turn world affairs around and bring everlasting peace for a thousand years is shown in the next few chapters. God's Will and purpose will stand. Many will ultimately receive eternal life.

Apocalypse

Chapter 15

The Wrath of God

Revelation 15:1

"And I saw another sign in Heaven, great and marvelous: seven angels with the seven last plagues; for in them is filled up the wrath of God."
(Revelation 15:1, MKJV)

Why is God angry? Why bring punishment on people? Why would God allow the earth to bring forth plagues? We will discuss this first.

Understand that God gave mankind a pristine paradise to live in. Humans could have enjoyed the fruits of paradise for thousands of years. Life could have been picturesque, exciting, and bountiful. Nobody would ever have to experience hunger, disease, or crime. It was all good, very good, and only good.

"And God saw everything that He had made, and behold, it was very good. And the evening and the morning were the sixth day."
(Genesis 1:31, MKJV)

Humans simply had to maintain paradise. That's all.

"And Jehovah God took the man and put him into the garden of Eden to work it and keep it."
(Genesis 2:15, MKJV)

But humans must love, appreciate, worship, and follow God's guidance.

"but you shall not eat of the tree of knowledge of good and evil. For in the day that you eat of it you shall surely die."
(Genesis 2:17, MKJV)

Instead, humans disregarded God's clear instructions. They wanted to do their own thing. They would throw the instruction book away and mess around as they pleased. Instead of living in beautiful villages, humans built concrete jungles filled with crime and filth. These are surrounded by polluting factories, causing disease and death to animals and, ultimately, humans. Even the animals in the sea suffer death by the pollution of single-use plastics, strangling the life out of sea creatures created by God.

Many prophets were sent to plead with humans. Many prophets were sent to the supposedly holy people of Israel, but they were often ridiculed, persecuted, and even killed.

"Therefore, behold, I send prophets and wise men and scribes to you. And you will kill and crucify some of them. And some of them you will scourge in your synagogues and persecute from city to city;
so that on you may come all the righteous blood shed on the earth, from the blood of

righteous Abel to the blood of Zechariah the son of Berachiah, whom you killed between the temple and the altar."
(Matthew 23:34-35, MKJV)

Jesus, the very Son of God, was condemned by the very priesthood that was supposed to know the scriptures and should have recognized Him, but they were knowingly ignorant. Even the Roman Empire's justice system failed Him. Even Herod, a politically connected Arab from the East, wanted Him dead from the beginning. Today, Christian evangelists are jailed and sometimes killed in some countries. Even in supposedly "Christian" countries, pastors are jailed for refusing to marry gay couples! The daily prayer was removed from public places. Christian education in schools was banned!

Why would God protect these people and the leaders they chose from diseases and pandemics?

God desires Godly offspring.

"Therefore put to death your members which are on the earth: fornication, uncleanness, passion, evil desire, and covetousness (which is idolatry),
on account of which things' sake the wrath of God is coming on the sons of disobedience,"
(Colossians 3:5-6, MKJV)

We have seen in some countries how even youngsters are being indoctrinated to accept the fornication of the LGB+ lobby group, enforcing their ways onto society. They will bring diseases into communities. The sin of people and wayward leaders has polluted God's creation.

The same creation will bring forth plagues, and God's wrath will be on people. He will allow the suffering. We were warned. So understand that God is justified to allow His wrath on polluting, corrupt people who persecute His prophets, evangelists, and pastors.

Revelation 15:2

"And I saw as it were a sea of glass mingled with fire. And those who had gotten the victory over the beast, and over his image, and over his mark, and over the number of his name, stand on the sea of glass, having the harps of God."
(Revelation 15:2, MKJV)

What is the "sea of glass?"

"And a sea of glass was in front of the throne, like crystal."
(Revelation 4:6, MKJV)

The sea of glass indicates the transparency of God's ways. Our sins can hide us from God, and so He also becomes an enigma to us, but that is not the way God wants it to be. In the Garden of Eden, humans sinned and then hid from God. However, the saints can understand God through much Bible study and repentance of sin. Once purified of guile and deception, the saints can stand before God's throne. The space available before God's throne is also huge. There is space for everyone who wants to stand before God. The fire usually indicates purification, sometimes through trials, if needed. Those who reach God's throne have studied and exposed the deception of false worship. They have uncovered the false religion and indoctrination that some governments (particularly beastly world empires) have developed and forced onto the population. They have overcome the sin of the cities, and have mental power over the wiles of Satan.

Revelation 15:3

"And they sing the song of Moses the servant of God, and the song of the Lamb, saying, Great and marvelous are Your works, Lord God Almighty, just and true are Your ways, O King of saints."
(Revelation 15:3, MKJV)

The "Song of Moses" can refer to the song the Israelites sang after God saved them from slavery by the Egyptian army, when He opened the Red Sea for them, and they walked through the middle of it. See below:

"Then the sons of Moses and Israel sang this song to Jehovah, and spoke, saying, I will sing to Jehovah, for He has triumphed gloriously; the horse and his rider He has thrown into the sea.
Jehovah is my strength and song, and He has become my salvation. He is my God, and I will glorify Him, my father's God, and I will exalt Him.
Jehovah is a Man of war; Jehovah is His name.

Pharaoh's chariots and his army He has
thrown into the sea; his chosen captains also
are drowned in the Red Sea."
(Exodus 15:1-4, MKJV)

The saints have overcome the beast power of the world empire. Through faith in Jesus Christ and understanding His supreme sacrifice for sin, the saints have also overcome personal sin. They sang these songs as they admitted that God and His Son empowered them to overcome deception and sin. They are also extremely grateful that God saved them from death by the world's sin and crime, as well as wars. Even if they died by disease or old age, they will still be resurrected at the return of the Messiah.

But there is more to the song of Moses and Jesus Christ. God called the Israelites to serve Him. They promised to keep the Commandments, the statutes, and the precepts. They promised to keep the whole Law of Moses. Christians also promised to keep the Commandments and enacted the New Covenant by the blood of Jesus Christ. Furthermore, Christians also understand that aspects of the Law must still be kept, such as hygiene, diet, human conduct, the preservation of life, and charity. They studied and obeyed these, and understood that God's way preserves life and is marvelous. These songs continue to praise God's ways of righteousness as taught through His laws

Revelation 15:4-5

"Who shall not fear You, O Lord, and glorify
Your name? For You only are holy. For all
nations shall come and worship before You,
for Your righteousnesses were made known."
(Revelation 15:4, MKJV)

Now the second vision of Revelation 15 continues. It refers to God's Tabernacle, where He comes to be among humans. It refers to the Testimony of the Covenant, the tablets with the Ten Commandments.

"And after these things I looked, and behold, the temple of the tabernacle of the testimony was opened in Heaven."
(Revelation 15:5, MKJV)

This is explained in the Bible. When Moses established the Godly religion for the Israelites during the Exodus, the Tent that would become the Tabernacle had to be precisely formed, as it was patterned after the Heavenly reality. See Hebrews 8. We will consider the earthly pattern:

"And on the day that the tabernacle was reared up, the cloud covered the tabernacle, even the tent of the testimony. And at evening it was upon the tabernacle, looking like fire, until the morning.
So it was always. The cloud covered it, and it looked like fire by night."
(Numbers 9:15-16, MKJV)

In this "Temple of the Tabernacle of the Testimony" was the Ark of the Covenant with the Ten Commandments. God is adamant that His Commandments must be kept always. It is the basis of His righteousness.

Revelation 15:6-8

Nations ignore Godly worship. Even some governments are corrupt and ignore Godly worship. Because some religious organizations and even "Christian" churches ignore the Ten Commandments contained in the Tabernacle, disasters arise. Society fails. Governments fail. Churches fail. Ultimately, God is not obliged to intervene and prevent failures.

"And the seven angels came out of the temple, having the seven plagues, clothed in pure and white linen, and were tied at the breasts with golden bands.
And one of the four living creatures gave to the seven angels seven golden vials full of the wrath of God, who lives forever and ever.
And the temple was filled with smoke from the glory of God, and from His authority. And no one was able to enter into the temple until the seven plagues of the seven angels were completed."
(Revelation 15:6-8, MKJV)

Chapter 16

Seven Vials

We will now see how societies fail in the Last Days and why.

"And I heard a great voice out of the temple saying to the seven angels, Go and pour out the vials of the anger of God on the earth." (Revelation 16:1, MKJV)

The First Vial

The first vial will allow pandemics to spread. The disregard for God's Word and the breaking of many laws in the Bible will cause this. The Bible prescribes specific laws concerning hygiene, clean and unclean food, and farming methods. Farming of unclean animals should be prohibited. Experiments in labs with unclean animals can lead to worldwide pandemics. Humankind in general totally ignores this, to our own hurt.

"And the first went and poured out his vial on the earth. And a bad and grievous sore fell on the men who had the mark of the beast, and on those who worshiped his image." (Revelation 16:2, MKJV)

Indoctrinated people will go to war for the beast government. Some believe in Communism, Capitalism, or Socialism. And they also have some form of religion that is not strictly from God's Word, yet they will want to enforce their ideas on religion. They and their families worship the image of a society put forth by mere people, or dictators and despots. Sores mentioned here can be on the outer skin or even the lungs or intestines, as these are in some ways an extension of the human skin. Due to disregard for God's Word, pandemics are prophesied. Notice the law given to God's society when they left Egypt during the Exodus.

> "And it shall be, if you will not listen to the voice of Jehovah your God, to observe and to do all His commandments and His statutes which I command you today, all these curses shall come on you and overtake you.
> Jehovah shall strike you with lung disease and with a fever, and with an inflammation, and with an extreme burning, and with the sword, and with blasting, and with mildew. And they shall pursue you until you perish."
> (Deuteronomy 28:15, 22, MKJV)

Historical events such as the Spanish flu demonstrate the risks of disease transmission during wartime. Currently, there is concern that research on viral warfare could result in accidental leaks and potential pandemics. Additionally, the spread of infectious diseases among military personnel during deployment remains a public health concern.

"Flee fornication. Every sin that a man does is outside the body, but he who commits fornication sins against his own body."
(1 Corinthians 6:18, MKJV)

Yet the mark of the beast is forcing peoples to accept the fornication of LGB+ people as normal. This is clearly against the Law of God. Therefor God will allow diseases to come on society. But will they learn to worship and obey their Creator?

The Second Vial

"And the second angel poured out his vial on the sea. And it became like the blood of a dead one, and every living soul died in the sea."
(Revelation 16:3, MKJV)

According to scriptural teachings, the consumption of blood is prohibited. Blood is described as containing the life of the flesh, as well as being associated with the consequences of sin and, consequently, disease. The phrase 'the sea becomes blood' is interpreted to mean that the sea has become diseased, rendering its fish unsafe for consumption and potentially fatal. But humans ignore God's direction to their own hurt.

"but that we write to them that they should abstain from pollutions of idols, and from fornication, and from things strangled, and from blood."
(Acts 15:20, MKJV)

This instruction was disseminated to all nations influenced by Christianity. However, many governments persecuted evangelists and subsequently established institutions that promoted doctrines asserting the abrogation of Biblical law, thereby diminishing the authority of the Word of God. Consequently, these nations are subject to the curses described for the Last Days.

Pollution is expected to result in the emergence of diseases. Major food sources may be depleted, potentially leading to conflicts among nations. Additionally, atmospheric pollution contributes to global warming and ocean acidification.

The Third Vial

Marine pollution and its detrimental effects are likely to extend to river systems, as contaminated rainwater disseminates pollutants worldwide.

"And the third angel poured out his vial on the rivers and fountains of waters, and they became blood."
(Revelation 16:4, MKJV)

Rivers and their fish became diseased, rendering another food source hazardous to human health and contributing to increased hunger and famine.

Some individuals may interpret these events as consequences of collective wrongdoing, questioning whether there is divine justification for such disasters in the eschatological context. Historical instances include the imprisonment of Christian evangelists for preaching, as well as legal actions against pastors who declined to officiate same-sex marriages due to their religious convictions. Additionally, some perceive the increasing recognition of other faiths by governments as contributing to the marginalization of Christian communities.

> "And I heard the angel of the waters say,
> Righteous is the Lord, who is, and was, and
> who will be, because You have judged these
> things,
> since they have poured out the blood of the
> saints and prophets; and You gave them blood
> to drink, for they were deserving.
> And I heard another out of the altar saying,
> Even so, Lord God Almighty, true and
> righteous are Your judgments."
> (Revelation 16:5-7, MKJV)

The Fourth Vial

The factors contributing to global warming are expected to intensify. Greenhouse gases emitted by large industrial complexes will trap heat that would otherwise escape the atmosphere. Increased volcanic activity, which would typically be moderated by a cooler atmosphere, is likely to release additional greenhouse gases. The melting of glaciers will expose extensive land areas at the poles, reducing pressure on the Earth's crust and facilitating further volcanic eruptions, which in turn will emit more greenhouse gases. Rising ocean temperatures in regions such as the Bermuda Triangle will transfer heat to substantial methane reserves beneath the seafloor, resulting in increased methane release into the atmosphere. These interconnected processes may create a self-reinforcing cycle that accelerates global warming.

"And the fourth angel poured out his vial onto the sun. And it was given to him to burn men with fire.
And men were burned with great heat. And they blasphemed the name of God, He having authority over these plagues. And they did not repent in order to give Him glory."
(Revelation 16:8-9, MKJV)

Because of environmental pollution, these plagues will affect cities and nations. It remains to be seen whether people will seek guidance from the Word of God, religious leaders, or biblical instruction.

The Fifth Vial

"And the fifth angel poured out his vial on the throne of the beast, and its kingdom became darkened. And they gnawed their tongues from the pain.
And they blasphemed the God of Heaven because of their pains and their sores. And they did not repent of their deeds."
(Revelation 16:10-11, MKJV)

This situation is causing significant damage to the world empire's capitals. The city and its industries are more directly impacted than other regions.

While the dominant power has waged war in various nations and cities, acts of terrorism are now occurring in its own capital. These attacks may involve conventional methods, but are likely to include biological and chemical weapons.

The dominant power has caused conflict and suffering globally, extracting resources and polluting many countries, which has led to widespread disease and hardship. Now, terrorism has reached its own capital.

The Sixth Vial

"And the sixth angel poured out his vial on the great river Euphrates. And its water was dried up, so that the way of the kings from the rising of the sun might be prepared."
(Revelation 16:12, MKJV)

The Euphrates River flows from Turkey through Syria into Iraq, where it joins the Tigris River before reaching the Persian Gulf. For eastern forces such as Russia and China to access the valley of Armageddon and potentially engage the EU over resources, the river would need to be dried up. Turkey and Syria have already constructed dams and diversion structures that allow them to control the river's flow. In the 1970s, these actions nearly led to conflict, as Iraq received insufficient water for agriculture. Turkey and Syria were eventually compelled to release enough water to meet Iraq's needs. In the event of a future famine, similar tensions could arise, potentially enabling military movements from Russia and China. Climate change and solar flares could accelerate this scenario.

"And I saw three unclean spirits like frogs come out of the mouth of the dragon, and out of the mouth of the beast, and out of the mouth of the false prophet."
(Revelation 16:13, MKJV)

If the river dries up, it is expected to cause significant concern within the EU. The term 'dragon' is associated with Satan, who is believed to motivate others to engage in conflict under the pretense of a just cause. The world government's leadership may use this situation to justify war and related actions. Additionally, some religious leaders may misinterpret scripture to support the prospect of war at Armageddon.

> "For they are spirits of demons, working miracles, which go forth to the kings of the earth and of the whole world, to gather them to the battle of that day, the great day of God Almighty."
> (Revelation 16:14, MKJV)

These events pertain to the Last Days. Christians are encouraged to remain steadfast in their faith, endure adversity, and prepare for the Messiah's return, so they may serve in the coming Kingdom of God. It is important to remember that the exact time of Christ's return is unknown. Christians should continue to study, worship, obey, and seek personal purification.

> "Behold, I am coming as a thief. Blessed is the one who watches and keeps his garments, lest he walk naked and they see his shame."
> (Revelation 16:15, MKJV)

Some governments may attempt to elevate other faiths and religions to the same level of rights as Christianity. While Christians are generally peaceful, they may not recognize threats to their religious freedom until they experience oppression. If Christians are pressured to compromise their faith, they risk losing their spiritual integrity and may forfeit their place in the Kingdom of God.

"And he gathered them into a place called in the Hebrew tongue Armageddon."
(Revelation 16:16, MKJV)

Given the catastrophic consequences of the preceding events, nations are likely to compete for scarce resources. Many populations may also turn to religious beliefs, hoping for divine intervention.

Major world powers are expected to assemble their military forces in the valley of Megiddo, located north of Israel. The drying of the River Euphrates will enable armies from the east (including Russia, China, and Iran) to join forces against those from the north and west (NATO) and the south (Israel and certain Arab states). Control over this strategically significant region will determine access to vital resources, including oil, gas, and food. Maritime access through the seas surrounding Israel will be essential for large vessels. Additionally, significant gas reserves are anticipated to be discovered off the coasts of Israel and Lebanon. Jerusalem holds religious significance for Jews, Christians, and Muslims, further intensifying the situation. Heightened religious fervor is likely to drive efforts to secure rights, maintain access to resources, and facilitate free trade to avert global economic collapse.

The Seventh Vial

The final catastrophe will now play out around Megiddo. It will be a disaster for the Middle East. However the catastrophic event extends well beyond a mere city. It extends to other cities. It even extends to the religious sphere.

> "And the seventh angel poured out his vial into the air. And a great voice came out of the temple of Heaven, from the throne, saying, It is done!
> And voices and thunders and lightnings occurred. And there was a great earthquake, such as has not been since men were on the earth, so mighty and so great an earthquake." (Revelation 16:17-18, MKJV)

Unlike the previous vials, this one is thrown into the air, symbolizing religious consequences that will be discussed further.

A major earthquake is expected in the Middle East. Industrial extraction of oil and gas is releasing pressures that have stabilized the region's crust for millions of years, increasing the risk of widespread seismic activity. This could result in the destruction of many cities and disrupt supply lines from the east for the armies at Armageddon.

> "And the great city came to be into three parts, and the cities of the nations fell. And great Babylon was remembered before God, to give to her the cup of the wine of the anger of His wrath.

And every island fled away, and mountains
were not found."
(Revelation 16:19-20, MKJV)

Babylon fell in the past and was never fully rebuilt. Today, it is primarily an archaeological site under excavation. In prophecy, Babylon is often cited as the origin of false religion. Here, Babylon is referenced as a symbol, and a future world empire may attempt to restore former worship practices. The next chapter will address this topic.

The great Asian tsunami demonstrated that earthquakes extending into the sea can generate massive waves capable of overrunning or even moving islands. In some cases, islands may sink, resulting in significant loss of life. Landslides can also reduce mountains to hills. Spiritually, this may symbolize the eventual disappearance of religious groups as people recognize that their beliefs cannot save them. Mountains can also represent governments that collapse due to corruption and the suffering of their populations.

"And a great hail, as the size of a talent, came
down out of the heaven on men. And men
blasphemed God because of the plague of the
hail; for the plague of it was exceedingly
great."
(Revelation 16:21, MKJV)

After an earthquake, dust from destroyed cities can linger in the atmosphere. These particles may collect moisture in the cold upper layers, forming hailstones that can damage crops and endanger people and animals.

As an introduction to the next chapter, note that Babylon developed a false religion in opposition to true Godly faith. Elements of these beliefs remain today, and for God's Kingdom to reach all people, these Babylonian systems must be removed.

The ruins of Babylon are located in present-day Iraq. Babylon was founded by Nimrod, who rejected God and established a city and religion based entirely on human ideas and laws.

"And Cush fathered Nimrod. He began to be a
mighty one in the earth.
He was a mighty hunter before Jehovah.
Therefore it is said, Even as Nimrod the
mighty hunter before Jehovah.
And the beginning of his kingdom was Babel,
and Erech, and Accad, and Calneh, in the
land of Shinar."
(Genesis 10"8-10, MKJV)

Babel was the origin of confusing ideas and manmade worship systems that oppose or "go before" God. Therefore, God confused the language of Babel and prevented further development. However, the concept and desire for Babel eventually led to the development of Babylon. The confusion of religious ways simply continued and opposed God on every level. The city had a main temple called "Bel" or "Babel". The city housed the original "Ishtar Gate". The form of this "Ishtar Gate" was duplicated in the old Germany in which Hitler formed his political movement. Ishtar is the goddess of love and war.

Ishtar was also worshiped in the Roman Empire, around the time when Christianity spread to Rome. It was celebrated in the spring, around the same time as Passover, instituted by God. To eliminate the dispute in the Roman Empire between the pagans and Christians, Emperor Constantine combined the two religious practices, calling it Easter. But the modern Easter is not celebrated on the right date sanctioned by God, nor are the right practices. The tradition of the egg is not in the Bible. The falseness of Babylon even extends to the world today, where many churches make these mistakes. Hence, God is still dealing with "Babylon".

Chapter 17

Eliminating Babylon

The full realization of God's Kingdom on earth, along with humanity's enjoyment of its associated benefits, safety, and peace, is depicted as contingent upon the elimination of Babylon. Opposition to God and the Messiah is presented as a barrier that must cease. Obedience to God's Commandments is characterized as essential for sustaining an ideal society. Additionally, the cessation of exploitation and pollution of creation, as well as the end of false religion, are identified as necessary conditions.

Chapter 17 illustrates the empire's eventual failure in opposing God's way as explained and ratified by Jesus Christ. Additionally, it demonstrates the downfall of the manmade religion established in opposition to the faith originating from Jerusalem. The chapter further details the specific manner in which this failure will occur.

The previous chapter identified certain failures. In the current section, the actions of the sixth and seventh angels, who administer the final two vials, are described in greater detail. These passages elaborate on the activities of antichrist movements and their attempts to undermine authentic Christianity.

"And one of the seven angels who had the seven vials came and talked with me, saying to me, Come here, I will show you the

judgment of the great harlot sitting on many
waters,
with whom the kings of the earth committed
fornication, and became drunk with the wine
of her fornication, those inhabiting the earth."
(Revelation 17:1, MKJV)

In biblical prophecy, a woman often symbolizes the
church; in this context, she represents a false church. This
entity is depicted as engaging in spiritual fornication and
potentially condoning physical fornication. The narrative
highlights corruption between church and state, with the
false church leveraging state power to oppress authentic
Christianity and offering superficial spiritual favors, such
as condoning sin. She claims to be composed of priests of
God and asserts the authority to forgive sins, a power
attributed solely to Christ. Furthermore, she enables
governments to manipulate public opinion, motivating
individuals to wage war under the guise of a state-
sanctioned religious cause. Soldiers, misled by her
influence, may believe they are serving God by
participating in violence. The influence of this false church
extends across nations, with rulers utilizing her to justify
and enforce colonial domination as divinely sanctioned.
Thus, she is characterized as the spiritual harlot.

"And he carried me away into a desert by the
Spirit. And I saw a woman sitting on a scarlet-
colored beast, filled with names of blasphemy,
having seven heads and ten horns."
(Revelation 17:3, MKJV)

The beast is a ruthless government that allows the false
church to use it to oppose and destroy true Christianity.

This beast even had power over the Promised Land at times. The reference to the desert could indicate the desert area around the Promised Land.

> "And the woman was arrayed in purple and scarlet. And she was gilded with gold and precious stones and pearls, having a golden cup in her hand full of abominations and filthiness of her fornication.
> And on her forehead was a name written, MYSTERY, BABYLON THE GREAT, THE MOTHER OF HARLOTS AND OF THE ABOMINATIONS OF THE EARTH."
> (Revelation 17:4-5, MKJV)

Certain churches dress their officials in purple and scarlet garments. These institutions possess significant wealth, having received substantial financial contributions from individuals seeking favor or forgiveness from the priesthood. Additionally, they obtain considerable funding from governments, which enables them to influence and control public opinion. These churches have established similar institutions internationally, which remain subject to the same forms of external control.

> "And I saw the woman drunk with the blood of the saints and with the blood of the martyrs of Jesus. And when I saw her, I marveled with a great marveling."
> (Revelation 17:6, MKJV)

According to some interpretations, the so-called false church persecuted adherents of authentic Christianity and promulgated doctrines that justified these actions. It is argued that this institution misinterpreted and distorted various scriptures. Furthermore, it is suggested that the church influenced secular authorities, symbolized by the beast, to suppress those identified as true Saints who maintained the original Christian faith. The identity of this church, often referred to as the harlot who rode the beast, remains a subject of theological debate.

> "And the angel said to me, Why did you marvel? I will tell you the mystery of the woman and of the beast that carries her, that has the seven heads and ten horns."
> (Revelation 17:7, MKJV)

The Bible will now explain the vision.

> "The beast that you saw was, and is not, and is about to ascend out of the abyss and go into perdition. And those dwelling on the earth will marvel, those whose names were not written in the Book of Life from the foundation of the world, when they behold the beast that was, and is not, and yet is."
> (Revelation 17:8, MKJV)

Those who remain committed to the original faith of the first century will understand. Others influenced by differing beliefs may find this confusing.

"And here is the mind which has wisdom. The
seven heads are seven mountains, on which
the woman sits."
(Revelation 17:9, MKJV)

A governing structure in prophecy is often referred
to as a mountain. In ancient days governments and rulers
built their cities on mountains with high walls so that it can
be protected from enemies. It was their seat of power.
Another possibility is that the false church's buildings seem
to be built among seven hills.

"And there are seven kings; five have fallen,
and one is, and the other has not yet come.
And when he comes, he must continue a
short time.
And the beast that was, and is not, even he is
the eighth, and is of the seven, and goes into
perdition."
(Revelation 17:10, MKJV)

This prophecy has a parallel fulfillment. The five
kingdoms preceding John and the First Advent of the
Messiah were Egypt, Assyria, Babylon, Medo-Persia, and
Greece. The sixth, present during John's time, was the
Roman Empire, which would eventually fall.

The seventh empire may refer to the Ottoman Empire, a
Turkish Islamic caliphate that ruled over Israel before the
First World War. The Empire appointed a Muslim mayor in
Jerusalem and opposed Christian interests. The First World
War led to its collapse, but Islamic influence is expected to
reemerge as a challenge for Western powers.

A future, revived Roman Empire in Europe is
anticipated as the eighth world empire. It will resemble

previous empires, featuring a religion that appears Christian but is fundamentally pagan and ultimately opposed to Christian principles.

Additionally, the succession of Roman Caesars is relevant. By the time of John's writing, Julius, Augustus, Tiberius, Caligula, and Claudius had already died.

Nero, who ruled during John's time, set Rome on fire, blamed Christians, and persecuted many. He later attempted to rebuild the city according to his vision. Historical accounts suggest he suffered from severe mental illness, leading to his isolation until his death.

Galba succeeded Nero, but Rome entered a period of decline. This suggests a dual fulfillment of the prophecy. A future world power in Europe, reminiscent of the Roman Empire, is anticipated. Developments from the east may prompt nations to unite.

"And the ten horns which you saw are ten kings, who have received no kingdom yet, but will receive authority as kings one hour with the beast.
These have one mind, and they will give their power and authority to the beast."
(Revelation 17:12-13, MKJV)

It is unlikely that the ten kingdoms in Europe can be identified at this time. In the event of war, Europe's borders may be redrawn, leading to the emergence of ten leaders who could transfer authority to a central government, police force, and army. While this may initially appear peaceful, it could present challenges for Christians committed to preserving their faith. As in the era of Emperor Constantine, various faiths may be merged, and a unified belief system could be imposed throughout the region. Christians seeking to maintain the integrity of their beliefs may face significant difficulties.

> "These will make war with the Lamb, and the Lamb will overcome them. For He is Lord of lords and King of kings. And those with Him are the called and elect and faithful ones."
> (Revelation 17:14, MKJV)

Initially, the central government and police will suppress Christians who adhere strictly to biblical teachings and reject the hybrid faith promoted by the central church. This resistance will create internal unrest within their countries. Over time, these actions are expected to have negative consequences, including increased crime. Eventually, political leaders are likely to withdraw their support from the hybrid church.

> "And he says to me, The waters which you saw, where the harlot sits are peoples and multitudes and nations and tongues,
> and the ten horns which you saw on the beast, these will hate the harlot and will make her desolate and naked. And they will eat her flesh and burn her with fire.
> For God gave into their hearts to do His mind, and to act with one mind, and to give their kingdom to the beast until the Words of God will be fulfilled.
> And the woman whom you saw is the great city which has a kingdom over the kings of the earth."
> (Revelation 17:15-18, MKJV)

The hybrid church maintains a global presence. Initially, European governments may support the hybrid church, but this support is likely to dissipate change over time. The church, headquartered in a city known for its seven hills, may eventually need to withdraw to its base.

Chapter 18

Babylon is Fallen

In the Last Days false religion will fall.

The complete establishment of the Kingdom of God and the universal expansion of Jesus Christ's rule require the total eradication of false religion.

False religion frequently becomes entangled with commerce and wealth. In such cases, the state and religious institutions collaborate to pursue financial gain and political power. This dynamic is widespread. The state is then characterized as a beast, actively opposing authentic religious doctrine, while false religion is depicted as a spiritual harlot, engaging in bribery and corrupt dealings. As a result, pervasive corruption emerges.

Jesus Christ alone is regarded as entirely incorruptible, uniquely qualified to serve as both King and High Priest. Therefore, until His Second Advent, a complete separation between church and state is necessary.

Accordingly, Chapter 18 addresses the fall of Babylon, initially as a false religious entity and subsequently as a city that enables global commerce. Its downfall is described as beginning with the collapse of trade and governmental structures, ultimately culminating in a loss of faith as individuals recognize the extent of their deception.

"And after these things I saw another angel come down from Heaven, having great

authority. And the earth was lighted up from his glory.
And he cried mightily with a strong voice, saying, Babylon the great has fallen, has fallen! And it has become the dwelling-place of demons, and a prison of every unclean spirit, and a cage of every unclean bird which has been hated,
because of the wine of the anger of her fornication which all the nations have drunk. And the kings of the earth have committed fornication with her. And the merchants of the earth became rich from the power of her luxury."
(Revelation 18:1-3, MKJV)

The dual statement "has fallen, has fallen" indicates that false religion will again be misused in the Last Days, and it will utterly fail before the return of the Messiah.

Demons are depicted as presenting themselves as sources of light and truth, yet they distort doctrine and Biblical law, thereby permitting injustices. Furthermore, demons are described as instigating the formation of alternative religions. The illicit alliance between state and religion is characterized as fornication. This dynamic is accompanied by exploitative trade practices that enrich merchants while impoverishing the general population. Additionally, these actors are portrayed as exploiting the earth and disregarding divine laws intended to prevent environmental degradation.

Biblical texts propose an economic model centered on agriculture and family-owned farms. While urban development is acknowledged, the model emphasizes the necessity for individuals to retain access to untaxed family farms. According to these texts, slaves are to be emancipated every seven years, and every fifty years, families are permitted to reclaim lost farmland without financial obligation. This system is intended to prevent perpetual poverty among families, in contrast to contemporary socioeconomic conditions.

Leviticus chapters 25 to 27 outline these principles. Historically, these regulations have not been widely implemented by nations and were only enacted in the Promised Land during the reigns of righteous kings.

It is anticipated that upon the return of the Messiah, these principles will be instituted in Judea and subsequently extended globally.

"The Spirit of the Lord is on Me; because of this He has anointed Me to proclaim the Gospel to the poor. He has sent me to heal the brokenhearted, to proclaim deliverance to the captives, and new sight to the blind, to set at liberty those having been crushed,
to proclaim the acceptable year of the Lord."
(Luke 4:18-19, MKJV)

This will be done when Jesus Christ returns. This is one of many aspects that Messiah will implement. For this to happen, the world needs to be freed from false religion. The true saints are admonished not to accept false doctrine or become involved in the oppression of the poor and unfair trade practices. God wants to protect the saints from disasters, from sickness and pandemics. Over exploitation of the earth can bring hunger and disease. Individual Christian saints must stay pure from false religious practices to uphold the pure and true Gospel.

"And I heard another voice from Heaven,
saying, Come out of her, My people, that you
may not be partakers of her sins, and that
you may not receive of her plagues.
For her sins joined together, even up to
Heaven, and God has remembered her unjust
deeds.
Reward her as she has rewarded you, and
double to her double, according to her works.
In the cup which she mixed, mix double to
her.
As much as she has glorified herself and has
lived in luxury, so much torment and sorrow
give her. For she says in her heart, I sit as a
queen, and I am not a widow; and I do not see
mourning at all.
Therefore her plagues will come in one day,
death and mourning and famine. And she will
be consumed with fire, for the Lord God who
judges her is strong."
(Revelation 18:4-8, MKJV)

An ineffective economic model, influenced by
misguided religious ideologies, can lead to national decline.
Populations experiencing poverty, hunger, and illness may
ultimately undermine governmental institutions and
infrastructure that do not address their needs. In extreme
cases, this unrest may extend to the destruction of religious
buildings.

.

"And the kings of the earth who have
committed fornication and lived in luxury with

her will weep for her, and will wail over her
when they see the smoke of her burning;
standing afar off for fear of her torment,
saying, Woe! Woe to the great city, Babylon,
that strong city! For in one hour your
judgment came."
(Revelation 18:9-10, MKJV)

Religious and governmental structures are intended to
serve the broader population; however, in many countries,
these institutions primarily benefit the elite. Societal
judgment arises when such institutions contribute to
widespread poverty and desperation among the populace.

.

"And the merchants of the earth will weep and
mourn over her, for no one buys their cargo
any more;"
(Revelation 18:11, MKJV)

The list of goods no longer being traded is
mentioned. Some will be worth mentioning. Thyine wood
is found primarily in North Africa, as well as ivory.

"the cargo of gold, and silver, and precious
stones, and of pearls, and fine linen, and
purple, and silk, and scarlet, and all thyine
wood, and every ivory vessel, and every vessel
of very precious wood, and of bronze, and of
iron, and of marble,"
(Revelation 18:12, MKJV)

Spices are primarily from India.

"and cinnamon, and incenses, and ointment, and frankincense, and wine, and oil, and fine flour and wheat, and beasts, and sheep, and horses, and chariots, and slaves, and souls of men."
(Revelation 18:13, MKJV)

Another significant moral issue is human trafficking. This practice is widely condemned due to its inherent exploitation. The use of cheap labor during periods of economic growth, followed by abandonment and exposure to hunger, constitutes a serious ethical violation.

"And the fruits of the lust of your soul have
departed from you, and all the fat things and
the bright things departed from you, and you
will find them no more, not at all.
The merchants of these things, who were
made rich by her, will stand afar off because
of the fear of her torment, weeping and
mourning
and saying, Woe! Woe to the great city which
was clothed in fine linen and purple and
scarlet, and adorned with gold and precious
stones and pearls!
For in one hour such great riches was
desolated. And every ship-pilot, and all the
company on the ships, and sailors, and as
many as work the sea, stood afar off.
And they cried out, seeing the smoke of her
burning, saying, What is like the great city?
And they threw dust on their heads, and
cried, weeping and mourning, saying, Woe!
Woe to the great city, by which all who had

ships in the sea were rich out of her
costliness! For in one hour she was ruined.
Rejoice over her, Heaven, and the holy
apostles, and the prophets, since God judged
your judgment on her.
And one strong angel took up a stone like a
great millstone and threw it into the sea,
saying, So on an impulse the great city,
Babylon, will be thrown down and not at all
will be found any more.
And the voice of harpers, and of musicians.
and flutists, and of trumpeters will be heard
no more at all in you. And every craftsman of
any craft will not be found any more in you.
And the sound of a mill will never more be
heard at all in you.
And the light of a lamp will never more shine
at all in you. And the voice of the bridegroom
and of the bride will never more be heard at
all in you. For your merchants were the great
ones of the earth; for by your sorceries all
nations were deceived."
(Revelation 18:14-23, MKJV)

The merchants engaged in deceptive practices at the
expense of the poor. Efforts to preach true biblical
teachings were met with persecution. Consequently, divine
judgment and destruction are portrayed as justified
responses.

"And in her was found the blood of prophets,
and of saints, and of all those who were slain
on the earth."
(Revelation 18:24, MKJV)

Apocalypse

Chapter 19

Joy in Heaven

To understand Chapter 19, we need to be aware of what God's hope and divine Will have been for humans all along.

We could have lived in paradise or a utopian society. There could have been no crime. We could have had healthy, energetic bodies untouched by industry pollution. We could have had large, perfectly healthy families. Every person would have inherited a family farm not taxed by the government. Our religion would have been pure. God would be among us, and we would have no regrets about past sin. We all could have lived productive and fulfilling lives.

Instead, humanity makes its own rules. Many governments create laws as they please, even allowing corruption. The result is pollution, sickness, and disease caused by "clever" people and managed by central governments that play god. There are wars and rumors of war. The rich grow richer, and the poor go hungry. Farmlands are overexploited by industry syndicates, leaving the land barren. Tropical forests are destroyed, and carbon is not absorbed, causing global warming and fires.
The Angels of God had high hopes for the families of Adam and Eve, but Satan intervened, and the humans listened to the antichrist activist and his lies, and followed their own short-term desires.

Ever since then, there has been crime and destruction. All evil happened on the earth: human trafficking, enslavement, child sacrifice in clinics, and enrichment of the elite.

God called His nation to their Promised Land and told them how to live and manage their economy. Family farms were to exist. Slaves were to be released every seven years. A jubilee every 50 years would allow families to regain their farms freely. Nobody should go hungry or be a slave for long. The Law of God is in the Bible. But Israel did not fully implement it; instead, it made laws that override God's Law. They lost their Promised Land more than once and remain embroiled in wars to keep it. The time of the Messiah's return is near. God's Angels eagerly await the Messiah to end the madness of humans trying to rule themselves against God's Will.

God's plan of salvation has been happening anyway. Jerusalem was established against all odds and was ready to receive the ultimate Passover sacrifice as Jesus Christ came to demonstrate God's Will and Law in action, even when crucified for being right. Many saints have also learned God's righteousness and lived pure lives, pleasing God in all they do.

Therefore, understand that the Angels will welcome the return of the Messiah and the resurrection of the saints. They can't wait for God's intervention to bring peace to the earth. They can't wait for the ultimate peaceful manifestation of God's way. They gladly awaited the takeover from Heaven to restore utopia to the earth.

> "And after these things I heard a great sound of a numerous crowd in Heaven, saying, Hallelujah! Salvation and glory and honor and the power to the Lord our God!"
> (Revelation 19:1, MKJV)

The first problem that must be rectified is the establishment of the only real and true religion.

"For true and righteous are His judgments.
For He has judged the great harlot who defiled the earth with her fornication, and He has avenged the blood of His servants out of her hand.
And secondly they said, Hallelujah! And her smoke rose up forever and ever."
(Revelation 19:2-3, MKJV)

All false religions will disappear once the Messiah appears in heaven. His supernatural return will end all arguments.

"And the twenty-four elders and the four living creatures fell down and worshiped God sitting on the throne, saying, Amen! Hallelujah!
And a voice came out of the throne, saying, Praise our God, all His servants, and the ones fearing Him, the small and great.
And I heard as the sound of a great multitude, and as the sound of many waters, and as the sound of strong thunders, saying, Hallelujah!
For the Lord God omnipotent reigns!"
(Revelation 19:4-6, MKJV)

God will eventually rule the earth and all its governments and institutions through Jesus Christ. He will resurrect the saints to help Him in this achievement.

"Let us be glad and rejoice and we will give glory to Him. For the marriage of the Lamb has come, and His wife has prepared herself. And to her was granted that she should be arrayed in fine linen, clean and white. For the fine linen is the righteousness of the saints." (Revelation 19:7-8, MKJV):

Please note the following:

1) The saints are required to prepare themselves actively. The belief that no action is necessary is incorrect. They must engage in the study of the Bible and address the misconceptions propagated by false religions. Furthermore, they are tasked with demonstrating the existence of God and affirming the enduring validity of the Ten Commandments. These commandments form the foundation of the New Covenant, established through the sacrifice of Jesus Christ, and constitute a permanent way of life, including observance of the Sabbath command.

2) The process by which saints attain righteousness requires deliberate effort. An initial emotional response, such as singing hymns of praise, may serve as a starting point. However, saints must also cultivate the ability to act justly before both God and others. This is achieved through diligent study of scripture, adherence to divine law, and seeking guidance from the Spirit of Wisdom for proper understanding. According to prophecy, those who follow this path will participate in the first resurrection at the return of the Messiah.

"And he said to me, Write, Blessed are those who have been called to the marriage supper of the Lamb. And he said to me, These are the true sayings of God.
And I fell at his feet to worship him. And he said to me, See, do not do it! I am your fellow servant, and of your brothers who have the testimony of Jesus. Worship God, for the testimony of Jesus is the spirit of prophecy."
(Revelation 19:9-10, MKJV)

The Angel regards himself as a fellow servant of God and identifies the saints as brothers and sisters. This perspective signifies an elevation in status for the saints during the first resurrection.

"And I saw Heaven opened. And behold, a white horse! And He sitting on him was called Faithful and True. And in righteousness He judges and makes war."
(Revelation 19:11, MKJV)

Jesus Christ consistently adhered to the will of God and faithfully observed the Law. He did not condone sin, but instead engaged in discussions regarding the Law's application, demonstrating a correct and compassionate understanding of God's will. As both a legal authority and High Priest, He exemplified mastery of the Law. According to theological interpretations, when nations and armies attempt to attack Jerusalem to remove Him, He will be justified in responding through supernatural means. Spiritually, He is described as opposing false religion through His teachings.

"And His eyes were like a flame of fire, and on His head many crowns. And He had a name written, one that no one knew except Himself."
(Revelation 19:12, MKJV)

His gaze is so unwavering that any sinner must avert their eyes. He will be crowned as ruler over many nations, exercising both civil and religious authority. Furthermore, the scope of His dominion surpasses common expectations.

"And He had been clothed in a garment dipped in blood, and His name is called The Word of God."
(Revelation 19:13, MKJV)

He was crucified and assumed the roles of High Priest and King through His own sacrifice, demonstrating loyalty to God and enduring love for humanity. He possesses complete knowledge of the Bible, having participated in its composition and establishment.

"And the armies in Heaven followed Him on white horses, clothed in fine linen, white and clean.
And out of His mouth goes a sharp sword, so that with it He should strike the nations. And He will shepherd them with a rod of iron. And He treads the winepress of the wine of the anger and of the wrath of Almighty God."
(Revelation 19:14-15, MKJV)

Throughout history, leaders of various nations have persecuted individuals identified as true saints and faithful evangelists. According to Christian doctrine, Jesus will not show mercy to those who restrict the freedom to evangelize, which is viewed as essential for the salvation of individuals from sin. It is further asserted that Jesus will establish and enforce the Law of God as the immutable constitution governing all nations.

"And He has on His garment, and on His thigh a name written, KING OF KINGS AND LORD OF LORDS."
(Revelation 19:16, MKJV)

During His First Advent, Jesus called those who studied the scriptures and recognized Him as the Messiah to be followed. He led them to greater spiritual growth. He permitted rulers to persecute and ultimately execute Him, thereby revealing the moral failings of their governments.

At His Second Advent, such events will not recur. Jesus will return to rule on earth, and cooperation from kings and rulers will be expected. The general populace will support Him and insist that their leaders learn from Jesus Christ. Nevertheless, the initial response from some authorities may be to deploy military force against Him. This attempt will not be permitted, and those armies will face the dire consequences.

"And I saw one angel standing in the sun. And he cried with a great voice, saying to all the birds that fly in mid-heaven, Come and gather together to the supper of the great God,
so that you may eat the flesh of kings, and the flesh of commanders, and the flesh of strong

ones, and the flesh of horses, and those sitting on them, and the flesh of all, both free and slave, both small and great.
And I saw the beast, and the kings of the earth and their armies, being gathered to make war against Him who sat on the horse, and against His army.
And the beast was taken, and with him the false prophet doing signs before it, (by which he deceived those who had received the mark of the beast), and those who had worshiped his image. The two were thrown alive into the Lake of Fire burning with brimstone.
And the rest were slain by the sword of Him who sat on the horse, it proceeding out of His mouth. And all the birds were filled from their flesh."
(Revelation 19:17-21, MKJV)

The depiction of a sword emerging from Christ's mouth is intended to be interpreted figuratively. Only Christ is portrayed as possessing the authority to speak words that penetrate and expose evil or misguided intentions. Birds of prey typically tear flesh and then depart. In a figurative sense, individuals will lose the motivation to continue with the war. They will cease their efforts and may even turn against their leaders and generals. Consequently, the leadership will realize they have lost all influence over the populace. Any authority previously held will dissipate rapidly, much like mist vanishes before the sun or birds scatter from trees at sunrise

Chapter 20

Satan Destroyed

Following the elimination of all false religions by Christ, primarily as a result of His supernatural and powerful manifestation, a significant challenge will remain for the millennial reign of the Messiah.
Satan will continue to attempt to deceive humanity.

Therefore, in order to facilitate the Messiah's establishment of a global utopia, it is necessary for Satan and his demons to be isolated. According to scriptural promises, God will accomplish this at the Second Advent of Jesus Christ.

Revelation 20:1-3

"And I saw an angel come down from Heaven, having the key of the abyss and a great chain in his hand.
And he laid hold on the dragon, that old serpent, who is the Devil and Satan, and bound him a thousand years.
(Revelation 20:1-2, MKJV)

This period marks the commencement of paradise for all humanity. The millennial rule of Christ begins in earnest. During this thousand-year era, Satan will be restrained as the world witnesses a remarkable transformation, with peace established among all nations and families.

"And he cast him into the abyss and shut him up and set a seal on him, that he should deceive the nations no more until the thousand years should be fulfilled. And after that he must be loosed a little time."
(Revelation 20:3, MKJV)

Now follows a description of the events at Christ's return. On that day, saints who are alive will be glorified and rise to meet Christ in the air or the first heaven. Saints who lived and died over the past 6000 years will be resurrected with glorified bodies and raised to join the meeting with Christ.

Revelation 20:4-6

To support Christ, resurrected and glorified saints who have demonstrated their devotion and loyalty over millennia will be granted the opportunity to dwell in a utopian society and guide others toward God. They will possess complete freedom to evangelize and express their worship of God, as well as instruct others in following Jesus Christ, without fear of opposition or persecution. No individual or government will hinder their efforts. Authentic worship will extend to every region of the earth and reach every individual.

"Behold, I speak a mystery to you; we shall not all fall asleep, but we shall all be changed; in a moment, in a glance of an eye, at the last trumpet. For a trumpet shall sound, and the dead shall be raised incorruptible, and we shall all be changed.

For this corruptible must put on incorruption,
and this mortal *must* put on immortality."
(1 Corinthians 15:51-53, MKJV)

"For the Lord Himself shall descend from
Heaven with a shout, with the voice of the
archangel and with the trumpet of God. And
the dead in Christ shall rise first.
Then we who are alive *and* remain shall be
caught up together with them in *the* clouds, to
meet the Lord in the air. And so we shall ever
be with the Lord."
(1 Thessalonians 4:16-17, MKJV)

God's Law will be established. Individuals will be
allocated family farms, and the Jubilee system will be
instituted. All labor will endure and directly benefit those
who perform it. Land will not be subject to taxation.
Corruption between business leaders and government
officials will be eliminated. The earth will be protected
from overexploitation by industrial leaders, and pollution
will cease.

People will experience health and happiness as a result
of the saints' effective governance. Justice and fairness will
prevail, and crime will be eradicated. Former practices of
greed, exploitation, and false worship will no longer exist.

"And I saw thrones, and they sat on them,
and judgment was given to them. And I saw
the souls of those who had been beheaded for
the witness of Jesus and for the Word of God,
and who had not worshiped the beast nor his
image, nor had received his mark on their

foreheads, nor in their hands. And they lived and reigned with Christ a thousand years." (Revelation 20:4, MKJV)

The resurrected saints are described as ruling over the small number of individuals who remain alive at that time. The population will have been significantly reduced by wars, disease, and hunger during the great tribulation and wars of the Last Days.

Initially, only a small fraction of the population will survive these events; however, a utopian era is expected to follow, characterized by the absence of war. The remainder of humanity who died over the millennia will participate in the general resurrection, which is anticipated to occur one thousand years later.

"But the rest of the dead did not live again until the thousand years were finished. This is the first resurrection." (Revelation 20:5, MKJV)

The translation may be subject to misinterpretation. The text suggests that the saints participate in the first resurrection, which all happens on one day, when Christ returns in glory. All other individuals that ever lived are included in the later general resurrection, which takes place a thousand years later. This is also referred to the second resurrection. However, the second resurrection does not happen in one day. It is a general period of resurrections, spread out over several years. People are resurrected to fleshly bodies, as they will still be subject to the second and final death, unless they repent.

"Blessed and holy is he who has part in the
first resurrection. The second death has no
authority over these, but they will be priests
of God and of Christ, and will reign with Him
a thousand years."
(Revelation 20:6, MKJV)

The saints in the first resurrection are resurrected
into immortal spiritual bodies. They will no longer face
death every day. No earthly accident can kill them. No
person with any weapon can kill them. They will live and
rule with Christ a thousand years to build utopia and spread
paradise. The normal population alive after the wars will
live, marry, have children and gracefully grow old without
pain, having the joy to see their children and grandchildren
grow up before them. However, they will peacefully and
mercifully die and be resurrected later.

(For a detailed discussion on the resurrections, see the
following book:
Life after Death

https://www.amazon.com/Life-after-Death-Pieter-Voges-
ebook/dp/B08CL3ZG1B/ref=sr_1_11?dchild=1&keywords
=pieter+voges&qid=1596618605&s=books&sr=1-11)

Revelation 20:7-9

Now follow a period leading up to the end of the
millennial reign of Christ. At the end, a general or second
resurrection will happen. These were the general population
that engaged in continual sin, ultimately crime, even
destruction of people and properties, and ultimately war.
They will be resurrected with all their false religious ideas

and be steeped in sin. They may still cause a disaster for those who lived in utopia in the end. This cannot happen.

Those who grew up in utopia towards the end of the millennial rule of Christ will not know how false religions can lead to war and destruction. They will be so gullible. Resurrected criminals will easily ruin their society. So the gullible utopians must experience how sin happens. They must see it develop from the deception of Satan to false religions to conflicts, wars, and violence. They must be hardened to fiercely oppose those resurrected criminals and false teachers.

> "And when the thousand years have expired, Satan will be loosed out of his prison.
> And he will go out to deceive the nations which are in the four quarters of the earth, Gog and Magog, to gather them together to battle. The number of them is as the sand of the sea.
> And they went up over the breadth of the earth and circled around the camp of the saints, and the beloved city. And fire came down from God out of Heaven and devoured them."
> (Revelation 20:7-9, MKJV)

The purpose of this is for all the gullible utopians to understand that they must protect their freedoms in Christ. They must act against sin brought on by resurrected wayward people. They must all oppose false religion. They must resist Godless evil. Then the world will be ready to help those in the second resurrection let go of sin, forget false religion, and follow Jesus Christ in the worship of God, their Creator. They must resist any compromise with true worship, for the sake of maintaining utopia and saving those in the general and second resurrection.

Revelation 20:10

Those who are young and lived at the end of the millennial rule of Christ have now seen false religions and war again. They are ready to stand up for Christ. They are ready to argue against false leaders and preachers. They are ready and able to defend utopia. All the sinners, criminals, and war people of the previous 6000 years can be resurrected. Satan will be thoroughly suppressed.

"And the Devil who deceived them was cast into the Lake of Fire and Brimstone, where the beast and the false prophet were. And he will be tormented day and night forever and ever."
(Revelation 20:10, MKJV)

Revelation 20:11-15

All people that ever lived for thousands of years in the past will now have an opportunity to learn the truth about the real religion of Jesus Christ. Everyone will have the opportunity to learn and follow the way of Christ. All people will finally have a chance at salvation, notwithstanding past ignorance and being drawn into sin. They can learn and grow in the grace of Christ. They abhor their past life with urgency and seriousness. They can totally repent and prove how they have become a new people, rooting out sin in their lives. The mercy and love of

God provide a period of final grace to reach out to salvation and eternal life.

> And I saw a great white throne, and Him sitting on it, from whose face the earth and the heaven fled away. And a place was not found for them.
> And I saw the dead, the small and the great, stand before God. And books were opened, and another book was opened, which is the Book of Life. And the dead were judged out of those things which were written in the books, according to their works.
> And the sea gave up the dead in it. And death and hell delivered up the dead in them. And each one of them was judged according to their works.
> And death and hell were cast into the Lake of Fire. This is the second death.
> And if anyone was not found having been written in the Book of Life, he was cast into the Lake of Fire."
> (Revelation 20:11-15, MKJV)

If people don't repent in the good times of Godly worship, where Jesus Christ is understood as the only Messiah, then they will never repent. If they have not repented and are not thoroughly convinced of the Christian way as the only way, they cannot be saved. Neither can they be allowed to live and continue to cause harm and destruction.

This period of the general and second resurrection can be as long as a hundred years. It happens at the end, or even after the seventh millennium. It culminates with the New Jerusalem. Isaiah also prophesied about it:

> "For, behold, I create new heavens and a
> new earth. And the things before will not
> be remembered, nor come to mind.
> But be glad and rejoice forever *in that*
> which I create; for behold, I create
> Jerusalem a rejoicing, and her people a
> joy.
> I will rejoice in Jerusalem, and I will
> rejoice in My people; and the voice of
> weeping will no more be heard in her, nor
> the voice of crying be heard in her.
> There will not be an infant, nor an old
> man that has not filled his days. For the
> child will die a hundred years old; but the
> sinner *who is* a hundred years old will be
> despised."
> (Isaiah 65:17-20, MKJV)

Children who died tragically early in a previous life will be resurrected and have a full life to learn and prove the Christian way. Then they will worship God and follow Christ. They can die peacefully in old age but be changed into immortal beings. Adults will probably be resurrected later in the hundred-year period and have a few decades to experience the true faith and repent. They will also die peacefully and be transformed into immortal beings. However, some people who were present at Jesus's First Advent had all the knowledge, saw the wonders, and witnessed the coming of the Holy Spirit on Pentecost in Jerusalem, yet still rejected the gift of God, will have no possibility of repentance. Some will be resurrected at the end of the hundred years to be judged and left to die the second death.

Jesus provided a parable to explain the possibility that a few people already had all the opportunity for repentance and salvation, and deliberately squandered it knowingly and willfully.

Consider this parable:

Jesus raised Lazarus from the dead and healed him, and his family worshipped him. Yet there were incredibly rich Pharisees and Sadducees who acquired great wealth from the faith they distorted and developed around the Temple services. They had the scriptures. They knew better. They saw the coming of Jesus Christ. They saw the miracles. They heard His sermons. Yet they conspired and had Him crucified. What else can be done for them? They can only be resurrected at the end and receive judgment and condemnation as promised. They will still be unrepentant. No sorrow is detected in their souls. Their only sorrow is their fear of the final end.

Abraham was resurrected at the beginning of Christ's millennial rule. He is now resurrected and immortal with a glorified body. He assisted Christ in producing utopia for the whole world. He is known by all and greatly respected.

This rich man is resurrected after the millennial reign of Christ and at the end of the hundred years of the general resurrection. He remains mortal and unrepentant. Even knowing of the resurrected and eternally glorified Christ cannot move him to abhorrence of his past deeds in having the perfect and sinless Jesus crucified. The motivation was probably to maintain his lavish lifestyle, even if it meant having a totally innocent and holy man killed by the most cruel and gruesome method.

"But Abraham said, Son, remember that
you in your lifetime received your good
things, and likewise Lazarus evil things.
But now he is comforted and you are
tormented.
And besides all this, there is a great
chasm fixed between you and us; so that
they desiring to pass from here to you
cannot, nor can they pass over to us from
there.
And he said, I beg you therefore, father,
that you would send him to my father's
house,
for I have five brothers, so that he may
testify to them, lest they also come into
this place of torment.
Abraham said to him, They have Moses
and the Prophets, let them hear them.
And he said, No, father Abraham, but if
one should go to them from *the* dead, they
would repent.
And he said to him, If they do not hear
Moses and the Prophets, they will not be
persuaded, even though one rose from *the*
dead."
(Luke 16:25-31, MKJV)

The rich man is clearly unable to face Jesus Christ
or to communicate with him. The breach of trust was
severe and impossible to heal. A possible relationship with
God the Father was even more out of the question. Hence,
the rich man could only talk to Abraham.

Apocalypse

It is important to understand that the promises of the Messiah's coming were given to Abraham. The only recourse of the doomed rich man was to try to placate Abraham, but that is inadequate. A further point is that a true understanding of salvation implies the keeping of the Commandments given by Moses, and merely knowing of Jesus does not grant eternal life to anyone.

Chapter 21

Permanent Establishment

Following the return of the Messiah and the first resurrection, false religions are eliminated, and Satan is bound and restrained. The millennial reign of Christ then commences. At the conclusion of this period, the world witnesses the consequences of Satan and his followers once more, allowing humanity to address those involved in the second and general resurrection. While many will repent, some will not and will consequently be eliminated.

At this stage, God the Father is able to return to earth and re-establish a permanent dwelling, fulfilling the original intention for Adam and Eve and, to a lesser extent, for Israel.

During the millennial rule of Christ, environmental pollution was eradicated. Factories no longer emit toxic smoke, and waste is no longer disposed of into rivers and seas.

"And I saw a new heaven and a new earth. For the first heaven and the first earth had passed away. And the sea no longer is."
(Revelation 21:1, MKJV)

The old earth, heaven, and sea were not replaced but rather restored and renewed. Following the earthquakes, the Mediterranean Sea may have receded.

This passage may also serve as a spiritual metaphor for humanity's experience on earth, navigating the seas, and contemplating the vastness of the sky. Consider also that, figuratively speaking, a "sea" in prophecy sometimes refers to a massive number of soldiers, and hence this may also indicate that boats full of soldiers will never approach Israel via the Mediterranean Sea.

At this stage, God the Father can establish a permanent presence on earth. A new physical structure will be constructed, and a spiritually pure, heavenly world government will commence operations in Jerusalem, where God and His angels will reside.

> "And I, John, saw the holy city, New Jerusalem, coming down from God out of Heaven, prepared as a bride adorned for her Husband.
> And I heard a great voice out of Heaven saying, Behold, the tabernacle of God is with men, and He will dwell with them, and they will be His people, and God Himself will be with them and be their God.
> And God will wipe away all tears from their eyes. And there will be no more death, nor mourning, nor crying out, nor will there be any more pain; for the first things passed away.
> And He sitting on the throne said, Behold, I make all things new. And He said to me, Write, for these words are true and faithful."
> (Revelation 21:2-5, MKJV)

God the Father is presented as the foundational cause of the universe's existence. According to this perspective, He intends for humanity to eventually inhabit other planets. Repentant and faithful individuals are now believed to possess detailed knowledge regarding the stewardship of a pristine Earth and the maintenance of peace among themselves.

God the Father is described as referring to righteous individuals as His children. These individuals are considered the siblings of Jesus Christ, who is regarded as the first to be redeemed approximately 2,000 years ago.

"But now Christ has risen from the dead, and has become the firstfruit of those who slept." (1 Corinthians 15:20, MKJV)

God is now present in Jerusalem permanently. Only righteous and loyal individuals remain, as sinners have been eliminated. Furthermore, Satan and his demons have been banished permanently.

"And He said to me, It is done. I am the Alpha and Omega, the Beginning and the End. To him who thirsts I will give of the fountain of the Water of Life freely.
He who overcomes will inherit all things, and I will be his God, and he will be My son.
But the fearful, and the unbelieving, and the abominable, and murderers, and whoremongers, and sorcerers, and idolaters, and all liars, will have their part in the Lake burning with fire and brimstone, which is the second death."
(Revelation 21:6-8, MKJV)

One of the angels seeks to reveal to John the bride of Christ, identified as the saints who endured suffering for the name and purpose of Jesus Christ, the High Priest.

The bride of Christ, residing in the New Jerusalem, comprises individuals from the twelve tribes of Israel and from other nations, collectively forming the complete bride.

"And one of the seven angels who had the
seven vials full of the seven last plagues came
to me and talked with me, saying, Come here,
I will show you the bride, the Lamb's wife.
And he carried me away in the Spirit to a
great and high mountain and showed me that
great city, the holy Jerusalem, descending out
of Heaven from God,
having the glory of God. And its light was like
a stone most precious, even like a jasper
stone, clear as crystal."
(Revelation 21:9-11, MKJV)

We need to understand why God refers to all the wonderful crystal clear precious stones. The character and loyalty of the ruling saints are such that they hide nothing from God. They form a transparent government structure, and God sees that as precious stones. Therefor He will also have their residence built with precious crystal clear stones.

"And it had a great and high wall, with twelve
gates. And on the gates were twelve angels,
and having names inscribed, which are the
names of the twelve tribes of the sons of
Israel:

From the east three gates, from the north three gates, from the south three gates, and from the west three gates.
And the wall of the city had twelve foundations, and in them were the names of the twelve apostles of the Lamb.
And he who talked with me had a golden reed to measure the city and its gates and its wall.
And the city lies four-square, and the length is as large as the breadth. And he measured the city with the reed, twelve thousand stadia. The length and the breadth and the height of it are equal.
And he measured its wall, a hundred and forty-four cubits, according to the measure of a man, that is, of an angel.
And the foundation of its wall was jasper; and the city was pure gold, like clear glass.
And the foundations of the wall of the city had been adorned with every precious stone. The first foundation, jasper; the second, sapphire; the third, chalcedony; the fourth, emerald; the fifth, sardonyx; the sixth, sardius; the seventh, chrysolite; the eighth, beryl; the ninth, topaz; the tenth, chrysoprasus; the eleventh, hyacinth; the twelfth, amethyst.
And the twelve gates were twelve pearls. Respectively, each one of the gates was one pearl. And the street of the city was pure gold, as transparent glass.
And I saw no temple in it, for the Lord God Almighty is its temple, even the Lamb.
And the city had no need of the sun, nor of the moon, that they might shine in it, for the

glory of God illuminated it, and its lamp is the Lamb."
(Revelation 21:12-23, MKJV)

This crystal clear form of government will also extend to other nations through the resurrected saints of other nations.

"And the nations of those who are saved will walk in the light of it; and the kings of the earth bring their glory and honor into it.
And its gates may not be shut at all by day, for there shall be no night there.
And they shall bring the glory and honor of the nations into it.
And there shall in no way enter into it anything that defiles, or any making an abomination or a lie; but only those who are written in the Lamb's Book of Life."
(Revelation 21:24-17, MKJV)

Chapter 22

Completion

The Angel now concludes the message and vision authorised by God the Father and sent by Jesus Christ which was relayed by His Angel to John.

"And he showed me a pure river of Water of Life, clear as crystal, proceeding out of the throne of God and of the Lamb."
(Revelation 22:1, MKJV)

No longer will there be death and destruction. No longer will creative effort be wasted. Everything done will have a lasting and creative effect.

"In the midst of its street, and of the river, from here and from there, was the Tree of Life, which bore twelve fruits, each yielding its fruit according to one month. And the leaves of the tree were for the healing of the nations.
And every curse will no longer be; but the throne of God and of the Lamb will be in it, and His servants will serve Him.
And they will see His face, and His name will be in their foreheads."
(Revelation 22:2-4, MKJV)

The worship of the Creator God will be foremost in His creation. Therefor they live forever. Sinners will cease to have effect, even if it means that they cease to live.

"And there will be no night there. And they
need no lamp, or light of the sun; for the Lord
God gives them light. And they will reign
forever and ever."
(Revelation 22:5, MKJV)

The Word and the Law of God is a light to a
righteous, productive, and everlasting life, lived in peace
and prosperity.

"And he said to me, These sayings are faithful
and true. And the Lord God of the holy
prophets sent His angel to show to His
servants the things which must shortly be
done."
(Revelation 22:6, MKJV)

Now a message from Jesus Christ:

"Behold, I come quickly. Blessed is he who
keeps the Words of the prophecy of this
Book."
(Revelation 22:7, MKJV)

The Angel shows His humility before God and
Christ, and his fellowship with the apostle John.

"And I, John, saw and heard these things.
And when I heard and saw, I fell down to
worship before the feet of the angel showing
me these things.
Then he said to me, Behold! See, do not do it!
For I am your fellow-servant, and of your

brothers the prophets, and of those who keep the Words of this Book. Do worship to God. And he said to me, Do not seal the Words of the prophecy of this Book; for the time is at hand."
(Revelation 22:8-10, MKJV)

The time is at hand because all that is required for salvation has been accomplished. Jesus Christ, as the perfect and supreme sacrifice, now serves as our eternal High Priest in Heaven. We are called to follow His example, observing His balanced approach to God's Law, unwavering loyalty to God, and enduring love for those who choose to repent and pursue righteousness. Those who reject salvation will not be compelled to repent, nor will they receive eternal life. The harm they caused will not persist.

"He acting unjustly, let him still act unjustly. And the filthy, let him be filthy still. And the righteous, let him be righteous still. And the holy, let him be holy still."
(Revelation 22:11, MKJV)

Jesus promised to return, and reward His servants, who either preach and evangelise or support those who preach and evangelise with prayers and tithes.

"I am the Alpha and the Omega, the Beginning and the Ending, the First and the Last."
(Revelation 22:13, MKJV)

As per John 1:1, everything was created by God the Father through Jesus Christ. Everything on the earth was created for Jesus Christ, and His inheritance. He was there in the beginning, and He will return in the end, and make everything right again with God the Father.

The first thing for all humans is to keep the Commandments of God the Father.

"Blessed are they who do His commandments,
that their authority will be over the Tree of
Life, and they may enter in by the gates into
the city.
But outside are the dogs, and the sorcerers,
and the fornicators, and the murderers, and
the idolaters, and everyone who loves and
makes a lie."
(Revelation 22:14-15, MKJV)

Jesus will be King and Priest. He will be King of Jerusalem, the city secured and established by King David. But His rule will spread to the whole earth.

"I, Jesus, have sent My angel to testify these
things to you over the churches. I am the Root
and the Offspring of David, the bright and
Morning Star."
(Revelation 22:16, MKJV)

The invitation is to anybody to seek eternal life by being joined to the Body of Christ, the Church of God, who is the Bride of Christ, preparing herself for the spiritual marriage at Christ's return.

"And the Spirit and the bride say, Come! And
let the one hearing say, Come! And let the one

who is thirsty come. And he willing, let him take of the Water of Life freely."
(Revelation 22:17, MKJV)

The path to salvation is open. The Bible is complete. Nothing more needs to be done. The required prophecies have been fulfilled. More prophecies are happening. And the return of the Messiah and His millennial rule will happen.

A warning goes out to all humanity. Don't take away from the witness, the Bible. Don't do away with the Commandments. Don't preach lawlessness. Also, don't try to add to the Bible. There can be no further messiah. There can be no further prophecies. The Bible is complete and expansive.

"For I testify together to everyone who hears the Words of the prophecy of this Book: If anyone adds to these things, God will add on him the plagues that have been written in this Book.
And if anyone takes away from the Words of the Book of this prophecy, God will take away his part out of the Book of Life, and out of the holy city, and from the things which have been written in this Book."
(Revelation 22:18-19, MKJV)

Those who claim the Ten Commandments are no longer relevant, or who add to the Bible and present themselves as new messiahs, risk severe consequences as described in Scripture. These warnings appear in the final verses of the Bible, emphasizing their importance. At this point, we are encouraged to hope for the swift return of Jesus Christ to address the challenges of poor governance, corruption, unsustainable farming, epidemics, urban decline, crime, violence, and war.

"He who testifies these things says, Yes, I am coming quickly, Amen. Yes, come, Lord Jesus. The grace of our Lord Jesus Christ be with all of you. Amen."
(Revelation 22:10-12, MKJV)

For the apostle John, Jesus did come quickly. For all saints, Jesus will appear in their next conscious moment at the future resurrection. John died soon after sharing God's plan for humanity to love and worship Him, as did the other apostles and saints. Complete conversion and repentance lead to acceptance and eternal life. The earth will be restored to the paradise lost by Adam and Eve, giving everyone the opportunity to experience utopia and worship God.

The prophecy addresses humanity's initial rejection of God and His Son at Christ's First Advent. Humanity continues to be misled by manmade religions. Governments will rise and fall, often resorting to conflict to avoid inevitable failures in leadership.

Revelation outlines the events leading to the final world war, when humanity will seek the return of the Messiah. This will be followed by a promised millennium of prosperity, with Jesus Christ ruling alongside resurrected saints who remained loyal despite trials. Angels are depicted worshipping God as His Son restores the world and re-establishes paradise.

Ultimately, the world will be prepared for the physical resurrection of all who have died. Most will be rehabilitated and accept God's rule, receiving forgiveness through Jesus Christ and becoming children of God. Those who continue to reject God's care and authority, even after witnessing the transformation, will be allowed to die as the earth is cleansed of all human-caused pollution.

The future is certain and planned by God. It will be wonderful and will come to pass. In the meantime, expect governments to fail and manmade religions to be exposed. Continue to study God's Word, keep His Commandments, and learn His ways of peace and prosperity.

The future awaits the revealing of the saints …

www.ingramcontent.com/pod-product-compliance
Lightning Source LLC
Chambersburg PA
CBHW021954120726
47992CB00001B/258